THE G
PHILOSOPHY

William C. Soderberg

University Press of America,® Inc.
Lanham • New York • Oxford

Copyright 2000 by

University Press of America,® Inc.
4501 Forbes Boulevard, Suite 200
Lanham, Maryland 20706

12 Hid's Copse Rd.
Cumnor Hill, Oxford OX2 9JJ

Library of Congress Cataloging-in-Publication Data

Soderberg, William C.
The game of philosophy / William C. Soderberg.
p.   cm.
.Includes bibliographical references and index.
1. Philosophy—Introductions.   I. Title.
BD21.S617   1999   100—dc21   99-056791 CIP

ISBN 0-7618-1591-0 (pbk: alk. ppr.)

⊖™ The paper used in this publication meets the minimum
requirements of American National Standard for Information
Sciences—Permanence of Paper for Printed Library Materials,
ANSI Z39.48—1984

Contents

Acknowledgments

I wish first to thank a host of students who have joined me in trying to gain some insight into the game of life. At a recent celebration of Montgomery College's 50th anniversary, each country with students at the College was represented by a student carrying the country's flag. Over 150 flags were carried. This broad range of students has been an inspiration over the years as I have tried to develop an understanding of various cultural perspectives. I cite the names of students whose questions I have responded to on my web page. The address of the web page is www.clark.net/pub/soderber/philosophy.

I am also deeply indebted to many colleagues for their support and critical responses to my work. In particular, I thank Michael Eckert, Dianne Ganz, Myrna Goldenberg, Jennifer James, David Johnson, Tulin Levitas, Christina Okechukwu, Mary Owens, Matthias Schulte, Marvin Watts and Robert White. I also wish to thank the efforts of the College library staff who have provided invaluable support in the gathering of materials—especially Bonnie Favin and Harriet Reiter.

My family members have provided constant support. My wife Susan has reminded the readers of her history books that social games can collapse into civil war. Our children have played their parts as well. Keir's expression "we try to create a harmonious, more beautiful game" initiated the idea for the book's title, Anna has produced a more beautiful game on stage, and Jenka has created a family holiday, Inverted Pyramid Day. I thank my family for the encouragement they have provided and the many sacrifices they have undergone to permit me to complete this book. To each of my family members and to my parents Pat and Eileen, who showed me how to play the social game, I dedicate this book.

Prologue

Poets, songwriters, and philosophers have something in common. They search for images and metaphors that help us better to interpret and to deal with our world. These writers often seem to be having a great deal of fun.

Various philosophers have used the image of a game. This image is quite appropriate, since the creation of a fair social game has been one of the main goals of moral and political philosophy. The fun begins when the philosophers try to decide what is fair. In the search for an answer to what is fair, philosophers reflect the various answers that have been given by individuals and communities. Some people say that the rules are fair if they conform to the will of God, others claim that fairness is achieved when the order of nature is followed, and some say the game is fair if the rules are made democratically. Some hold that fairness requires an equal distribution of the wealth. Others simply throw up their hands and say that the game of life is not fair.

The philosophers' answers to what is fair shape as well as reflect the popular answers. The variety of answers has sometimes generated conflicts between different individuals and groups as well as conflicts within groups and within individuals. If there is any hope of overcoming the differences and managing the conflicts, the sources of the conflict must first be examined.

One source of conflict that philosophers face in the quest for a fair social game is the question of what makes the ordinary person tick. What, in other words, motivates people to action? As people watch and participate in games, they often gain insight into themselves and their motives. Some people may regard themselves as primarily self-interested, some may view themselves as benevolent individuals who place the interests of others before their own, and some may see themselves as mainly fair-minded persons.

The perspectives of self-interest, altruism, and fair-mindedness may be present in athletic contests. Some athletes may be motivated primarily by the self-interested desire to advance their own careers. Others may be genuinely benevolent or altruistic and place the interests of the team before their own. Referees are fair-minded and impartial when they properly perform their role in the game.

Philosophers reflect each of the three views. Some observe that self-interest need not be suppressed but that it must be properly channeled. Altruism produces cooperation, others claim, and cooperation can result in a team's success. A third group of philosophers claims that fair-mindedness keeps the game intact: the game can continue if the rules are agreed upon and fairly applied.

In this book, we will be observing philosophers deeply engaged in a game with a serious side. Like others involved in games, philosophers try to discover the goal of the game they are playing. Some say the goal of philosophy is practical, while others say it is speculative. The practical philosophers regard the role of philosophy mainly as problem management. The problem management approach sorts out the issue of how to deal with the world. The practical group spends a good deal of time trying to find a proper balance of self-interest, altruism, and fair-mindedness. On the other hand, the speculative philosophers often view the main role of philosophy as providing a representation or picture of the world. The speculative group places practical proposals regarding fairness on a foundation of answers to what is real and true.

This book is an invitation to you, the reader, to join in the philosophers' game. We will watch a give-and-take among philosophers as they debate the practical questions of what is right and good (morality) and what is just (political philosophy) and the speculative questions of what is real (metaphysics), what is true (epistemology), and whether God exists (philosophy of religion). My aim is to present the debates among philosophers from various traditions. In doing so I hope to support you in your own formulation of a fair social game and the related issues of what is good, right, just, real, and true. I invite you to join the philosophers in trying to discover the source of the rules in the social game and the purpose of the game of life itself. As an aid to comparing the philosophers' positions, I will employ the image of a card game throughout the book. To begin to understand this image or metaphor you may turn to Chapter One, in which I describe the Rawls Game.

PART 1:

MORAL AND POLITICAL PHILOSOPHY

Chapter 1: Some Preliminaries

Two major stories of moral and political philosophy have emerged in recent times. These two stories or theories provide markedly different views of the human person, morality and justice. The first is a communitarian story, the second a liberal tale. In the first, the human person is described as a social being; in the second, the person is viewed mainly as an individual. In the communitarian story, the good life or the kind of life worth living can be determined only within a community; in the liberal account, the good life or lifestyle is an individual matter. Several other features that we will examine distinguish communitarianism from liberalism.

These two stories seem to be so radically different that no reconciliation or common ground between them can be found. The first part of our project will be to grasp some of the main differences between the two stories and the power of each in its description of morality and justice. We will also consider how each story can collapse into a form of tyranny when, in the name of morality, some treat others in an arbitrary way. Our final concern will be to explore whether common ground may be found to allow adherents of each story to address differences and conflicts.

Both the communitarian and liberal stories have ancient roots in the history of ideas. In this book, some of the main roots will be examined. The communitarian account, as we will see, prevailed in the ancient and medieval worlds. With the emergence of moral liberalism in recent centuries, morality in many societies has become less a public and more a private matter. The liberal view is the major account of morality and justice in contemporary democracies. The rise of liberalism, according to its proponents, represents moral progress. The communitarian view, however, continues to have many adherents. Indeed, many individuals feel drawn toward both communitarianism and liberalism, so the conflict between the two stories can occur even within individuals.

Our study of the roots of communitarianism and liberalism will take us beyond the practical questions of morality and justice. Some philosophers who address moral and public policy issues also offer speculative answers to the questions of what is real and true. In the course of this work, various communitarian and liberal answers to these perennial questions of reality (metaphysics) and truth (epistemology) will be examined.

The Rawls Game

John Rawls is a major contemporary defender of a liberal notion of justice. One of Rawls' students, Ronald Green, devised a game to illustrate Rawls' conception of justice. Several classes of mine have played the game described in the following paragraphs. This version contains a few minor changes from Green's version.

The Rawls Game consists of three rounds. Prior to the first round I announce to the class that we are the elected representatives on the island republic of Nacirema. Each of us represents about one thousand constituents. Nacirema is a completely isolated island and the economy is agricultural. Everyone either farms or provides services to the farmers. The people own their own farms and believe strongly in looking out for number one. They also share the widespread belief that no one should be forced to do anything against his or her will. To protect liberty to the greatest extent possible, the legislature has adopted the procedure that all policy decisions must be adopted by unanimous vote.

The rules for the first round of the game appear on the blackboard: (1) you may look at the cards, and (2) the measure will pass if the vote is unanimous. I then pass out cards and explain the situation that we are voting on. The island has been afflicted with a serious drought and many, but not all, of its people are now suffering from the drought. The mountaineers have water from a snowcap on the mountain and continue to flourish. The flatlanders, who are completely dependent on rainfall for their crops, are suffering. The mountaineers make up about one-fifth of the population on the island. Those who have an "X" on their cards are mountaineers and those without a mark are flatlanders.

A proposal has been studied by our scientists and is now in front of the legislature for discussion and vote. The proposal is that water from the snowcap will be transferred equally to all farms on the island, and that an irrigation system will be built to make this possible. The mountaineers currently are living very well, since traditionally they have had an abundance of water for their crops. The flatlanders, however, even in the best of times have barely eked out an existence and in the present crisis are unable to do even that. In a few years, if the waterworks project is adopted, the unequal economic and social division between the mountaineers and flatlanders will be erased and everyone on the island—flatlanders as well as mountaineers—will be at the same economic level.

After some discussion and an exploration of alternative proposals, we bring this proposed waterworks project to a vote. Generally some of the mountaineers will vote against the proposal. When they do, I point out that a weakness is present in our system. We have followed the two procedures (looking at the cards and trying to get a unanimous vote) in an effort to protect everyone's liberty, but a tyranny of the powerful minority has resulted.

The second round of the game begins at this point. I entertain suggestions for changing either of the two rules of the game. The suggestion to have a majority vote is quickly made. I change the second rule to incorporate the suggestion. The two rules now read: 1) you may look at the cards; 2) the measure will pass if it receives a majority vote.

The situation for our second vote is as follows. A serious disease has broken out on Nacirema that takes the lives of ten percent of the population every year. Five people on the island have been found to possess an enzyme that protects them from the disease. Our scientists have also found that this enzyme provides a cure and prevents the disease in others who are vaccinated with the enzyme. After considering various alternatives, the scientists have determined that all five people must be hooked up to machines so that the enzymes can be extracted and used to bring the dreaded scourge to an end. The five people will have to be hooked up twenty-four hours every day for at least ten years–and perhaps longer.

Five representatives are given marked cards while the rest receive unmarked cards. Each of the representatives with a marked card has one constituent with the valuable enzyme. During the discussion of the proposal, the five representatives report whether their five constituents are willing to give consent. Sometimes the consent of the individuals is withheld until enormous sums of money are given; sometimes a small child is one of the people with the enzyme; and sometimes a constituent simply refuses to give up his or her freedom and rejects being attached to a machine. In the last case, the one who refuses is sedated and kept "happy" throughout the time that he or she is on the machine.

The vote is taken on the enzyme-extraction procedure, and generally a majority of the class votes in favor of the proposal. I then point out that a tyranny of the majority has occurred: the liberties of one or a few persons have been overridden for the good of the many.

The third round then begins. Again I invite a suggestion for a possible modification of the rules. Sometimes a student will suggest not looking at the cards. I take that suggestion and pass out a set of cards with the marks turned down, as I instruct the students not to look at the marks on the cards until after the vote is taken. In addition, I suggest that to protect the liberty of each person we return to the requirement that the vote be unanimous. The two rules now read: 1) you may not look at the cards; 2) the measure will pass if the vote is unanimous.

For the third round, another proposal faces the legislature. The proposal is that each mountaineer family will be assigned four flatlander families. If the mountaineers wish, they may provide food and shelter for their designated flatlander families. The flatlanders, meanwhile, are required to provide labor for the mountaineer farms. No wages are given for the labor, only food and shelter. The food and shelter are provided at the discretion of the mountaineer.

During the discussion of the proposal, someone invariably identifies it as a slave or serfdom proposal. When the vote is taken, the proposal is generally defeated with a unanimous vote. I then point out that we have adopted Rawls' perspective of justice and ruled slavery out. This procedure, according to Rawls, helps us to grasp the origin of a right not to be enslaved. We don't in "real life" actually engage in turning down the cards and voting unanimously; however, when we realize that such practices as slavery are not allowed in liberal societies, the image of the face-down cards can help us to grasp how and why they were ruled out. It is as if such a procedure were used. During the course of our study, we will see that the cards-down perspective has sometimes been associated with a religious point of view.

The link between religion and public policy is strong in the history of ideas. In Chapter Two we will examine different forms that this link has taken in various Mediterranean societies. One of our main projects is to gain some understanding of why the link between religion and public policy has been so strong. The central answer that we will explore is that many people believe war can be avoided if the cards are turned down before violence breaks out over issues that divide communities.

In Chapter Two, we will trace the link between religion and public policy through the traditions of Plato and Aristotle. Despite the problem of the tyranny of orthodoxy, as we will see, religion continues to exercise an influence on policy matters in many cultures. Modern liberalism has in large measure emerged as a corrective to the tyranny of orthodoxy that has historically accompanied the shaping of public policy by religious authorities.

In Chapter Four, "Modern Moral Liberalism," we will study classical and contemporary moral liberalism and review Rawls' efforts to preserve the strengths of both liberalism and communitarianism. We will examine Rawls' response to four major forms of tyranny–the tyrannies of the majority, the powerful minority, orthodoxy, and perfectionism. His response to the tyrannies of the majority and the minority is that the cards should be turned down for policy decisions, but Rawls is aware that the tyrannies of orthodoxy and perfectionism lurk nearby when the cards are turned down. We will see that Rawls addresses this problem with two main suggestions: first, the turning down of the cards is merely a hypothetical, not an actual, procedure; secondly, the cards may be regarded as inverted for some matters only. The fair-minded, cards-down perspective, Rawls maintains, helps to understand how individual rights are created. We will examine the matters for which Rawls would turn the cards down and review criticisms of his notion of a hypothetical social contract.

The three perspectives that emerge from the game will be helpful in our discussions of moral and political philosophies. The place given to self-interest, altruism, and fair-mindedness will be traced through various philosophies.

The central metaphor of the Rawls game—turning the cards face up for some decisions and face down for others—can be quite graphic to those who have played the game and expressed their intuitions on specific issues from the different perspectives. The card-game metaphor has its limitations, to be sure, so it will be used mainly to provide preliminary comparisons among moral theories in our search for a fair social game. It will also provide a framework for presenting some of the problems associated with various theories.

Moral Relativism: Survival of the Fittest

At this point in our search, you may be thinking that morality is simply an individual matter. Further, you might hold that so-called "morality" is simply a matter of conditioning. A person's beliefs and behaviors are best viewed as mere products of one's culture. The position that you are entertaining if you think along these lines is known as moral relativism.

In this section, I will talk about relativism and try to explain why it is so popular, but also why it quickly falls apart as a coherent story of the phenomenon that people call morality. We will then examine liberal and communitarian stories of morality. I will try to point out the important influence that relativism has exercised on these two major stories or approaches to morality.

As people become aware of practices in various cultures, many are led to the conclusion that what is right varies from culture to culture. Polygamy is practiced in some cultures, monogamy in others. Premarital relations are permitted in some cultures but foribidden in others. Some cultures are vegetarian while others are carnivorous. These and similar examples seem to provide evidence to support the assertion that what is right varies from community to community. They seem to support, in other words, a form of ethical or moral relativism that may be called communal relativism.

Communal (Cultural) Relativism: Horses in a Herd

Communal relativists hold that if a group regards an action as right, it is right. The group is the exclusive determiner of what is right. Communal or cultural relativism, may be illustrated with the image of a herd of horses. A dominant stallion provides protection for the mares and the young. There is no right or wrong in this animal herd; there are only hungry horses in need of food and protection. The survival of the herd increases the chances that each member of the herd will survive, so the good of the group and the good of each member of the group are closely connected.

Relativists regard humans as close to animals as far as questions of life's meaning and morality are concerned. Humans, like other animals, are subject to control and domination by others, and both human and non-human animals end their lives in the same way: they die. Non-relativists, on the other hand, regard humans as having capacities that fish and animals lack, capacities that make relationships among humans significantly different from relationships among non-human animals.

If the community is the determiner of what is right, a person who seeks to know what is right must only consult a community's standards. When the standards of different communities are examined, however, one quickly realizes that some pretty outrageous policies have been adopted at different times and places. Chattel slavery was practiced in various parts of the Americas for several centuries. Genocide has been inflicted on people of different religious or ethnic heritage in some European and other countries as recently as the twentieth century. To say a policy is right if a community or group declares it is right seems out of place or even misguided in light of such examples.

A search for a coherent response to communal relativism seems to point us in the direction of individual or subjective relativism. What is right, according to subjective relativists, varies from individual to individual. If an individual regards an action as right, according to the subjective relativist, it is right.

Individual (Subjective) Relativism: Fish in the Sea

The subjective or individual moral relativist regards the human person as an isolated individual who, independently of others, determines what is good and right. On this view, there are as many different standards of morality as there are people in the world. In effect, then, there is no shared standard of right action and no universal standard of right or wrong. A picture or model for this position is the model of fish in the sea, where big fish eat little fish. Individual relativists regard humans as quite similar to animals as far as moral and ultimate questions (questions about what is right, real, and so forth) are concerned. There is no measure of right and wrong; there are only hungry fish.

Subjective relativism can be tested and refuted in the same way that communal relativism has been challenged. Son of Sam, a mass killer in New York, claimed that mass killing was right–even divinely inspired. This claim runs counter to the ordinary intuitions of many people, who would hold that mass killing is wrong. To hold that mass killing is wrong, then, requires that one reject the claim of the subjective relativist that an action is right if an individual regards it as right.

Problems with contradiction and circularity also render moral relativism incoherent. The position of individual relativism may be expressed with this principle: "If a person regards an action as right, it is right." Along the same lines, the position of communal relativism may be expressed: "If a group regards a policy as right, it is right."

Philip Montague, a philosopher from the state of Washington, has pointed out that if two people have opposite opinions of an action, the consistent relativist must say that the action is right and it is wrong. This contradictory conclusion follows from the principle "If a person regards an action as right, it is right." The counterpart to this principle is "If a person regards an action as wrong, it is wrong." So, if one person regards an action as right and another person regards the same action as wrong, it follows from the relativist principle that the action is both right and wrong.

To avoid this apparent contradiction, people often modify the principle and say: "If a person regards an action as right, it is right in his or her view." Montague points out that if an action is right in someone's view, that person regards the action as right. Anyone who accepts this paraphrase, Montague observes, must acknowledge that the principle is equivalent to this statement: "If a person regards an action as right, that person regards the action as right." The principle is true but trivial. This circular principle tells us nothing about a state of affairs in the world. The effort to find consistency in a relativist principle leads first to contradiction and then to circularity. These are serious difficulties for moral or prescriptive relativists.

Examples of the sort we have been examining–known as "counter-examples"–help us to express our own intuitions; they ordinarily lead to the rejection of relativism in both its communal and individual forms. A plausible claim that may be made after the critical examination of both forms of relativism is that the individual and the community, in some combination, decide what is right. Neither the individual nor the community acting independently of the other is the exclusive determiner of right actions or policies.

The serious objections to relativism may well lead one to ask why relativism continues to be such a popular position. The reason may well lie in a failure to distinguish between descriptive and prescriptive relativism. Descriptive relativists hold that what is *regarded as* right varies. They may hold that what is regarded as right varies from culture to culture, or that what is regarded as right varies from individual to individual. The descriptive relativists may also hold that both of these claims are correct.

Prescriptive or moral relativists address the question of what is right. They hold that what *is* right varies. Prescriptive relativism takes two forms. These are the two positions reviewed above under the labels communal (or cultural) and individual (or subjective) relativism. Polygamy, slavery, genocide, and clitorectomy may be regarded as right in some times and places, but a person may still ask whether these practices are right.

The popularity of the view that morality is relative may now be explained in the following way. When people hold that morality is relative, they are ordinarily subscribing to a form of descriptive relativism. Descriptive relativism, in the judgment of many philosophers and non-philosophers, gives a highly plausible account of a state of affairs in the world.

Prescriptive relativists, however, make quite a different claim. They make the controversial claim that what is right varies from culture to culture or from individual to individual. While descriptive relativists give a description of an actual state of affairs, prescriptive relativists make a prescription about what could or should be. Descriptive relativism has been said to present claims about what is, but prescriptive relativism to make claims about what ought to be. The position of descriptive relativism can be readily verified through the study of different cultures or the observation of different individuals, but the claim of prescriptive relativism that what is right varies is highly controversial and requires defense. The popularity of relativism may be explained as the result of a failure to distinguish between descriptive and prescriptive relativism. The position that many people have in mind when they say "morality is relative" is descriptive relativism, not prescriptive relativism.

In the rest of this section and the remainder of the book, I will be concerned with prescriptive or moral relativism. When I refer to 'relativism' I will mean prescriptive relativism unless I specify otherwise.

The final objection to relativism is that moral relativists address only the question of who decides. When they address only this question, they fail to take into account other questions that people often ask in regard to moral issues: What is the standard of right action? What is the good life? Why be moral? What is virtuous? The failure to take into account these questions, along with the exclusive emphasis on the individual or the group and problems with contradiction and circularity, leads most philosophers to look elsewhere for a definition or standard of a right action or a good life. Some look to moral liberalism and others to moral communitarianism.

Neither moral liberalism nor moral communitarianism is a relativist position. Both positions assign a role to the individual as well as to the community in moral decision-making. In liberalism, the individual is the primary moral agent; in communitarianism the community is the primary agent. The main differences between liberals and communitarians, as we will see, may be traced to conflicting views of the human person and the source of personal identity.

Moral Liberalism and Moral Communitarianism

Over the years, moral philosophers have found many ways to describe the phenomenon that people call "morality." "Moral liberalism" and "moral communitarianism" are terms that have been used in recent decades as philosophers have tried to understand morality. Each of these two ways is reflected in different answers to the six basic questions related to morality that are discussed in this section. The divisions over these questions, in turn, are tied to divisions over questions concerning justice, reality, and truth.

Other terms and concepts have also been used to approach the complex phenomenon known as morality, but liberalism and communitarianism are terms that have served well to describe some of the major divisions among moral philosophers. Throughout the text, many subtleties and nuances of these two positions will be explored. In this chapter, some of the key differences between liberalism and communitarianism will be previewed.

Before studying the answers of the various philosophers, you could get into the spirit of the game of philosophy by writing down your own answers to these six questions. After you have done so, ask yourself whether each answer is consistent with your answers to the other five questions. As you search for consistency, you are beginning to engage in philosophy.

1. Who is the primary moral agent?

The popular form of this question is "Who decides?" When such thorny issues as abortion and euthanasia arise, we frequently hear people ask the question, "Whose decision is it anyway?" Four answers to the question of who decides are possible: the individual, the community, both, or neither is the moral agent. Individual relativists, as discussed in the previous section, hold that the individual is the exclusive moral agent, while communal relativists regard the community as the sole moral agent.

If a person holds that both the individual and the community decide, the issue then becomes who is the primary decision-maker or the primary moral agent. Liberal thinkers favor the individual as the primary moral agent, while communitarian thinkers lean toward the community as the primary moral agent. In answer to question 5 below ("Who determines the good life?"), the liberals reply that the individual decides the kind of life to lead, while communitarians hold that the community determines the more significant features of the good life.

The community is generally the possessor of rights in communitarianism, but the individual is the main possessor of rights in liberalism. The decision on what constitutes a right is a communal decision in both communitarianism and liberalism. Liberals accept that rights are created to avoid serious wrongs that divide communities.

If someone claims that neither the individual nor the community decides, the question then is who or what does decide. One common position in this case is that morality is based on divine revelation. A transcendent being or beings determines what is right and wrong, good and bad. This position in morality is known as a divine command theory.

Moral Liberalism. The individual is the primary moral agent. The individual creates his or her identity and determines the good life.

In one version of liberalism—that of John Rawls—the cards are turned down to define rights and the basic institutions of society. When great harms, injustices, and social division threaten, people are capable of adopting a fair-minded point of view. Reason prompts people to turn the cards down to create the basic human rights.

In another version of liberalism, utilitarianism, the individual determines the good life and the cards are never turned down. Great harms can be addressed through the feeling of altruism; they need not be addressed by turning down the cards to negotiate rights. Sympathy can prompt the relief of suffering; thus sympathy is the origin of basic rights designed to alleviate suffering. So utilitarians say that these rights are a product of feelings—namely, compassion or altruism—and not a product of reason.

Moral Communitarianism. The community is the primary moral agent. The individual takes his or her identity from the community. The community determines the good life from a cards-down perspective.

When the individual enters the moral picture, he or she always enters as a communal being. An individual may hold a conception of the good life, but this notion is shaped by the community's conception of the good.

Some moral communitarians hold that a transcendent God reveals the moral rules. This may be called a divine command theory of morality. A divine command theory typically states that a divine being is the primary moral agent. A divine command theory quickly defeats itself in the search for a coherent and consistent standard of morality. The claim that a transcendent being reveals moral truths is defeated when revelations conflict. When two groups claim divine revelation as the origin of their moral practices and the practices of one society directly conflict with those of another, the conflict can peacefully be resolved only by offering reasons why one revelation is superior to the other. The highest court of appeal, as it were, has already spoken. The appeal to reasons leads one to search for other accounts of morality. Divine revelation or divine command theories of morality are defeated by this objection since they cannot stand up to the tests of coherence and consistency. Debates related to these issues will be examined in detail in Part Three below, Philosophy of Religion.

2. What is the definition or standard of right action?

This question is the one that drives people to endless conversations and debates over morality, or it may have the opposite effect and reduce people to silence when they try to talk about moral issues. People have been looking for a way to measure right actions for thousands of years, but they have not agreed on how to do so. The difficulty of finding a standard or measure of right action leads many to conclude that morality is relative. Others are led by the difficulty to intensify the search for a moral standard that seems to be there but can only be glimpsed on occasion.

Moral Liberalism. The definition or standard, according to moral liberals, constitutes the universal principle of morality. The search for a universal standard is the primary moral issue for moral liberals. More important than the issue of a good or virtuous character is that of a right action. The action that a person performs rather than the character of the person is the main focus for moral judgments in liberalism. Liberals see the shift in the primary focus from good character to right action as moral progress.

Some liberals maintain that the results of an action determine whether it is right, while others hold that it is the kind of action that determines whether it is right. The utilitarians defend as the standard the greatest good of the greatest number. This standard addresses the consequences of an action: an action is right if it has beneficial results. Kantians, another group of liberals, offer a version of what they call "the categorical imperative" as the universal standard. Kantians look at the kind of action rather than the results of the action to determine whether it is right.

Moral Communitarianism. The question of the standard of right action, according to communitarians, is less important than the question of a person's character. The communitarians search mainly for a standard of goodness rather than of right action. The universal standard of morality for communitarians is the good life, not a single action. An action, according to the communitarians, is not detachable from the agent who performs the action.

3. *Why should I be moral?*

At some point in their lives–usually very early–many people make the interesting discovery that morality and the following of rules is fine, but only if other people follow the rules. In defense of this view, the following line of reasoning might be used. My society needs the moral rules to remain viable and survive. If it is to my advantage not to follow the rules, however, I will make an exception for myself and not follow them. Of course, I need to be careful not to get caught, since getting caught will not be to my advantage. My community, for example, might censure me for breaking the rules.

If individuals entertain the idea of making an exception for themselves, they are considering the possibility of being moral "free-loaders". As a moral freeloader, a person holds that morality is fine and may even follow the rules when they are in his or her favor. But when it is inconvenient or against one's interests to do so, the moral freeloader will carefully ignore the rules. Society won't fall apart, according to the moral freeloader, since most other people follow the moral rules.

The question "Why should I be moral?" is the same as the questions "Why should I not be a moral free-loader?" and "What is the motive of morality?"

Moral Liberalism. For some liberals feelings are the motive for morality, while for others the motive is the choice of consistent rules. Utilitarians answer that one should be moral out of sympathy for humanity. Concern for the welfare of others prompts me to follow the basic moral rule–namely, look out for the greatest good of the greatest number. Kantians answer that a person should follow the rules because he or she has chosen the rules.

Moral Communitarianism. The capacity to reason and gain knowledge distinguishes humans from non-humans and, according to communitarians, one should be moral to attain the human potential for reason or knowledge.

Platonists answer that one should be moral to attain knowledge of the higher Forms–especially the Form of the Good. Followers of the Platonic-Augustinian tradition during the Middle Ages added that people should be moral to fulfill the will of God. Some popular forms of Augustinian Christianity became divine command theories of morality.

Aristotelians hold that one should be moral to realize his or her potential. To attain virtue is to attain excellence, and in attaining excellence a person attains his or her potential. The unique potential for humans is the capacity to reason.

4. What is freedom?

'Freedom' is a slippery term. Its meanings are varied and reflect the wide range of views represented on the moral spectrum we have been exploring. While freedom is attractive both to liberals and communitarians, the meanings of the term are so different between each camp–and within each camp–that many moral disputes can be traced to the incompatible notions of freedom found among the different schools.

Moral Liberalism. Moral liberals place greater importance on the question of whether actions are free than on the question of whether a person is free. Freedom of the will is not a central issue for liberals.

Freedom for some moral liberals is an absence of constraint on the satisfaction of desires; for others it is the informed choice of the rules by which humans govern themselves.

Moral Communitarianism. Moral communitarians regard the issue of whether persons are free as more significant than the question of whether an action is free. Freedom of the will is a central issue for communitarians, since communitarians–as we will see in question 6 below–evaluate a person according to his or her intentional actions.

Among the ancient communitarians, freedom generally meant movement from a lower class of slaves to a class of citizens. The term was also used to designate a life in conformity with the community's notion of the good life. Knowledge of the good, on this view, would set one free. Finally, some communitarians regarded freedom as the exercise of the capacity to attain the potential given by heredity and environment.

5. *What is the good life?*

In popular culture, one may frequently hear the claim that morality is relative. The answer to the question of the good life that has emerged in moral liberalism seems to confirm in the minds of many that morality is relative.

Liberals regard the individual as the determiner of the good life. While the liberal seems to be close to relativism with this view, the liberal takes great pains to avoid relativism by claiming, as we saw in question 2 above, that a universal standard of right action may be discoverable. Some questions arise from this liberal stance: What is the right and what is the good? What is the relationship between the right and the good?

The question of the good involves several closely related issues. As an individual faces the question of life's meaning, several questions arise: What is the good life? What kind of life is worth living? What kind of lifestyle or career is worth pursuing? What is the meaning, purpose, or goal of life?

Moral Liberalism. Some moral liberals describe the good life as a life in which one's needs and desires are satisfied; for others it is a life in conformity with freely chosen rules. Utilitarians hold that the good life is one in which needs and desires are fulfilled. For utilitarians, the good takes priority over the right. This means that the policy most likely to produce the greatest good for the greatest number is right.

Kantians view the good life as one lived in conformity with freely chosen rules. For Kantians, the determination of the right precedes the determination of the good. This means that people consent to rules that can apply universally. Such rules determine what is right, since the rules seek to avoid serious wrongs in society. Within this framework, the individual is free to determine the good life.

Moral Communitarianism. For some communitarians the good life is a life in which one's potentials as a human being are realized.

Aristotelians generally accept self-realization as the standard of a good life.

The good life for many religious communitarians is life in conformity with the will of God. Those in the Augustinian tradition, for example, accept union with God as the good life. Augustine is interpreted by many as offering a divine command theory of morality. This interpretation seems accurate when applied to some of the popular versions of Augustinian Christianity.

6. What are the virtues or qualities of a good person?

The virtues are primary for moral communitarians, secondary for moral liberals. The evaluation of a person's character is of primary importance for communitarians, but moral liberals regard a focus on the evaluation of an action rather than a person's character as an advance in moral consciousness.

Moral Liberalism. A good character is not the main moral question for liberals. Liberals see too many problems with evaluating the person rather than the action. People, for example, can be condemned and cast out of a group for the actions they perform. To prevent such ostracism and to exercise tolerance, liberals focus their evaluations on actions. The liberals engage in much discussion of the standards by which to measure actions.

Moral Communitarianism. The question of virtue is the main moral issue for moral communitarians. More important than the issue of the standard of right action is the issue of a good or virtuous character. The character of a person is evaluated by communitarians since virtues are qualities that enable a person to get along in a community.

People who have separated themselves from a community by their intentional actions must follow certain procedures to restore themselves to the group. If the offense is small, an apology will serve the purpose. If the offense is great, a more severe penalty must be paid. Fines or even imprisonment for a time may be required before an offender can be restored to the community.

A Word about Logic

In the earlier section on relativism, positions have been criticized on the grounds that they are circular, contradictory, and so forth. This type of criticism will continue to appear throughout the text. Both the strengths and weaknesses of each position we examine will be identified.

Such terms as "circular" and "contradictory" are used in analyzing the logical consistency of arguments. One of the goals of philosophy is to try to make sense of various answers to the questions of what is right, good, just, real, and true. A way to make sense of an answer is to ask whether it is contradictory, circular, and the like. Logic may be used as a tool to help make sense of positions and arguments.

You may very well have doubts over applying logic to views on reality, morality, justice, truth, and religion. "These are simply areas," you might say, "where each view is just an opinion." As you entertain this notion, it may be worth asking whether all opinions are equally valid or equally well informed. If one person on a jury jumps to a conclusion about whether a person charged with a crime is guilty while a second juror carefully examines the evidence before making a decision, we may be inclined to place more trust in the second person's judgment. If someone holds the opinion that all persons outside of his own race are inferior, we may be strongly inclined to reject his opinion.

On what grounds do we reject some opinions but respect others? From a variety of past experiences, people have found that some issues can be more successfully addressed if a careful, thoughtful approach is taken. If a juror who jumps to a conclusion or a racist examines his or her assumptions, problems with their positions may become apparent. The tool of logic allows one to examine his or her assumptions. An assumption is a reason—often unstated—that supports a conclusion. Such an examination may reveal contradiction, circularity, faulty generalizations, or other problems.

Philosophers use logic as a tool to address various problems. For the most part, the philosophers don't claim that logic guarantees that their views are correct. Rather they turn to logic since it allows a more careful, thoughtful approach to the extremely difficult and complex problems addressed by philosophers. Such an approach, as past experience has often borne out, is more likely to give a successful resolution of a problem—in morality, justice, religion, and even in metaphysics and epistemology.

We rely on inferences for many of our day-to-day activities and claims. Inferences are built on assumptions. To determine whether an inference is acceptable, the assumption or assumptions on which it rests must first be identified.

One fairly direct method that can help to identify assumptions is to use an "if...then..." statement. The inference "His parents must be rich since he is a U. S. president" rests on the assumption "If someone is a U. S. president, he must have had rich parents."

With the assumption identified, its acceptability can be addressed. The statement "If someone is a U. S. president, he must have had rich parents" is equivalent to "All U. S. presidents have had rich parents." This general statement will be accurate or acceptable if there are no exceptions, but Abraham Lincoln and others may be cited as examples of presidents whose parents were not rich. These examples render the assumption unacceptable.

You may ask whether any assumption or generalization may ever be acceptable, and the answer is yes. For example, the inference "John F. Kennedy must have been a male, since he was a U. S. president" rests on the assumption "If a person has been a U. S. president, that person was (or is) a male." This is equivalent to the general statement "All U. S. presidents have been males." While someday this general claim may no longer be true, as of the date of this writing it is still an accurate general statement about past and present U. S. presidents.

One way to identify assumptions involves the following simple procedure. Place the conclusion of an inference in a "then" clause and the reason for the conclusion in an "if" clause. Then test the truth of the "if...then..." or conditional statement. If a claim of certainty is made, the conditional statement is a universal or general statement. This universal statement may then be checked to see whether the generalization holds true. For example, let's say the conclusion is "She must be a nurse." In this statement, certainty is claimed for the assertion that she is a nurse. The reason given for the assertion is "She is wearing a white uniform." The unstated assumption in the argument is: "If she is wearing a white uniform, she must be a nurse." This is equivalent to the general statement that "All people who wear white uniforms are nurses." The truth of this statement can be tested by citing examples of people who wear white uniforms but are not nurses. Navy personnel, chefs, and scientists may serve as counter-examples. A careful examination of assumptions often leads people to qualify the general claim. A more accurate claim in this case, for example, would be "She may be a nurse" or "She is probably a nurse." This qualification is important in critical thinking.

The "if...then..." procedure is one of the main approaches used to identify the assumptions of arguments or inferences. Other approaches are possible. Besides the conditional "if...then..." statement, the disjunctive "either...or..." statement could be used. The conjunctive "both...and..." statement could also be used. The approach generally used to identify assumptions in this text will be the conditional "if...then..." statement.

Identifying an assumption is the first step in a more careful or thoughtful approach to an issue. Such an approach may increase the chances of managing or even solving a problem.

We turn in the next chapter to the deep roots of communitarian thought in some Mediterranean societies.

Chapter 2: Ancient and Medieval Moral Communitarianism in the Mediterranean Area

When we move from relativism to the moral theories of communitarianism and liberalism, we move from the view that humans are simply like animals or fish to the notions that humans are capable of engaging in cooperative activity and that humans can attain more than mere survival. Humans build social structures in an attempt to achieve the complex goal of survival in freedom. Rather than engage in strictly individual activity or in blind subordination to a powerful leader, humans can cooperate in their efforts to attain both survival and individual freedom.

Communitarianism may be found in both strict and moderate forms. Strict or particular communitarianism encompasses various kinds of communities, including a "religious right." Plato and Augustine represent strict communitarianism in this chapter. Moderate or universal communitarianism may be regarded as a "communitarian left"; it moves in the direction of taking into account the interests of all members of the community. Aristotle, Maimonides, and Thomas Aquinas provide examples of moderate communitarianism.

Both strict and moderate communitarians regard the community as analogous to the human organism. In this model, the individual's survival is dependent on the survival of the community, just as the survival of each part of the body is dependent on the survival of the entire body. In strict communitarianism, the body is viewed as subordinate to the mind. Moderate communitarians, by contrast, regard the mind as having a closer alliance and harmony with the body.

Strict communitarians also hold that human society is like an upright pyramid. Different groups or classes play different roles in society. The rules are made by the one or the few at the top, who are believed to have greater knowledge of what is good, right, just, real, and true. A problem accompanies the pyramid model: when class division becomes too rigid, resentment sets in and the social pyramid collapses into a tyranny of orthodoxy with its arbitrary and impersonal treatment of people.

Communitarianism may be rescued from the tyranny of orthodoxy by a move toward the communitarian left. When challenges to the authority of the decision-makers in the upright social pyramid are raised, the decision-makers may preserve the pyramid by representing more fully the preferences of the people. This preservation is not accomplished without some cost: to protect the pyramid from the rigidity of a tyrannical orthodoxy, the pyramid must be inverted. This "inversion" is a way of expressing the idea that the rules take into account the interests and needs of the people. A difficulty with the inverted-pyramid model is that an inverted pyramid is unstable. Moral liberalism has emerged in efforts to stabilize the inverted communitarian pyramid. This liberal project will be examined in Chapters Three and Four.

The Platonic School: An Upright Social Pyramid

The moral communitarian regards the community as the primary unit in moral decision-making. According to the main ancient and medieval communitarians, the relationship of the individual to the community is analogous to the relationship of part of a body to the whole body.

Plato

Plato was a major figure in Western communitarianism. Plato rejected the relativist position, although he provided a detailed and sympathetic account of relativism in his writings. Plato lived during a period of corruption and turmoil in the democratic city-state of Athens, Greece. The state executed Plato's mentor Socrates. Plato had regarded Socrates as Athens' best citizen, and the trial and execution must have been a major factor in Plato's thinking about right and wrong. After Socrates was executed, Plato went into a period of exile. Later he returned to Athens and spent the remainder of his life working to bring about a just state that provided a place for political dissenters.

Plato gave a blueprint of a just state in his political utopia, *The Republic*. In this work, the just state is described as a state that is governed by the Guardians—fair-minded persons who have the welfare of all at heart. The military is subject to the Guardians, as are the merchants, craftsmen, and farmers. The loyal opposition and political dissenters, according to Plato, belong in the Guardian class. If they care enough to try to improve the state, political dissenters such as Socrates should be given the opportunity to act on their goals. Plato's conception of the just state may be pictured as an upright pyramid, with the Guardians at the top, the military immediately below the Guardians, and the merchants, craftsmen and farmers at the bottom of the pyramid.

Plato's conception of the just state is based on an analogy with a healthy individual. When reason directs the bodily appetites, the virtue of temperance is achieved; when reason directs the will, courage is present; when reason directs the intellect, wisdom is attained. When reason directs the intellect, will and bodily appetites, each part of the human organism plays its proper role and the virtue of justice is present. Inner harmony is the result.

Harmony within the state is achieved in a similar fashion. When the state--the "body politic"--is governed by the reasoning elements in the state, harmony or justice results. However, if the will (embodied by the military) or the bodily appetites (merchants, craftsmen, or farmers) take over the governance, disorder and injustice result. The merchants, craftsmen, and farmers are said by Plato to correspond to the bodily appetites in the body, since they look primarily to personal gain. The welfare of all in the society is not the primary concern of these private businessmen. The Guardians of the state, by contrast, are those who have demonstrated a concern for all and knowledge of how best to achieve fairness for all.

Plato describes a state governed by the reasoning elements as an aristocracy. The state can decline from the ideal of aristocracy when either the will or the bodily appetites take over. When the will--or military--takes over, timocracy develops. The leaders become more concerned about their reputations and preserving their power than fairness and the well being of all. The next stage of decline is plutocracy. The leaders in a plutocracy use public office for increasing personal wealth and the wealth of their families. The bodily appetites have overtaken the reason in a plutocracy. The next worse stage is democracy. When everyone wants an equal share of the wealth, the bodily appetites make things fall apart completely. To bring order of this chaos, a strong leader or tyrant emerges. Tyranny is the worst form of government and the final stage of the state's decline.

Only the few are capable of governing, according to Plato. In his ideal state, the few born with leadership qualities are selected early in life for extensive training. In regard to the Rawls Game, Plato's position is consistent with the view that only a select few are capable of turning the cards down. Those who are born with an ability to lead are the ones who have the ability to be fair-minded and invert the cards. Plato describes the individuals capable of leadership as persons who have gold in their veins.

The Guardians demonstrate their concern for everyone by denying themselves private families and private property. Wives and children were to be held in common among the Guardians. Plato compares family love, friendship, erotic love, and love of humanity and regards family love (*storge*) and erotic love (*eros*) as the types of love that bring humans closest to the animal world. Friendship (*philia*) and love of humanity (*agape*) are higher forms of love.

The knowledge of how best to govern is gained through the long period of training, during which the Guardians contemplate and through reflection gain knowledge of the Forms. They study art (beauty), science (truth), and moral philosophy (goodness). The highest Form is the Form of the Good. The dedication to the ultimate good on the part of the Guardians overcomes the conflict between the rich and poor—a conflict in the Greece of Plato's day that led to the deaths of many in civil strife.

One of the casualties of such strife was Socrates. In Plato's model of the just state, the dedication to goodness and fairness exemplified by such persons as Socrates was the catalyst that could bring about peace in the traditional conflict between the rich and poor classes.

Aristotle criticized Plato's view that only those with gold in their veins should serve as Guardians. Aristotle pointed out that the same people should always govern if Plato's claim that the leaders had gold in their veins—that is, that leadership is innate—were correct. Also see the criticisms of Plato by Lynda Lange and Susan Moller Okin in Chapter Nine below.

Plato regarded the Forms as permanent, nonphysical entities. Some of Plato's predecessors had proposed that everything could be understood in physical terms. Plato rejected this materialist account of reality. In addition, he rejected another account—idealism—which maintained that everything was nonphysical. Plato compromised, as it were, between the two and accepted a dualist view of reality. In Chapter Six, "Metaphysics," we will examine Plato's argument for the view that some things are physical and some nonphysical. Forms—such as the Form of the Good—were among the nonphysical things of the world. Everything in the physical world had a corresponding nonphysical Form.

Augustine

Several centuries after Plato's utopia, another major utopia that profoundly influenced the history of ideas was written by the African philosopher Augustine. As Plato's *Republic* before it, Augustine's *The City of God* was a product of a concern over injustice. In Augustine's case, however, the injustice occurred on a larger scale than that which Plato addressed. Some colonies on the fringes of the Roman Empire were treated harshly by the Roman military. Land distribution policies, for example, sometimes displaced indigenous peoples when the land was taken over by the Romans.

Resistance to this decimation of communities was mounted in some areas. In Palestine, for example, some Jews advocated violent resistance against Rome while others favored nonviolent resistance. Jesus Christ, who was probably regarded as a pacifist resister, was executed about forty years before Jerusalem was destroyed by the Romans in 70 A.D. and the Jews were thrust into dispersion. The establishment of the state of Israel in the second half of the twentieth century was the first Jewish state in the former Palestine in almost two millennia. The experience of the Jews and other colonists of Rome precipitated the movement known as Christianity, a movement for which Augustine became a central spokesperson.

In his *City of God*, Augustine contrasted the city of man with the city of God. The city of man was a society in which personal gain was valued over fairness and the welfare of all. The use of public positions for personal gain was a practice in the city of man and, according to Augustine, a practice that produced disorder. Such disorder was a feature of the colonialism of Rome, a military state that inflicted grave injustice in its failure to pursue a fair-minded treatment of all within the empire.

The city of God, on the other hand, was the community that based its policies on the advice of those who provided the voice of conscience in the state. Those who had suffered injustice were among the most valued members of the city of God. By coming together in voluntary associations, these individuals and others who sympathized with them could perform a valuable function in the state. Collectively they could act as the voice of conscience. This voluntary association, according to Augustine, was the church; as the conscience of the state, the church was the moral community.

In the Augustinian tradition of the Middle Ages, the members of the church directed the military leaders in the governing of a just state. The king or head of government was regarded as the head of the military. When the military leaders acted under the sanction of the religious community, a harmonious and lasting peace in the state was possible. The church was separate from the court or military when it played the role of conscience in the state. The different elements of the body politic played their proper roles when the military leadership derived its policy from the conscience of the state. When each part of the organism played its proper role, an inner harmony was present: justice and peace ensued when this mystical union of church and state was obtained. Such a state could be called a mystical body.

Augustine subscribed to the same set of virtues as Plato—wisdom, courage, temperance, and justice. To these Augustine added the Christian religious virtues of faith, hope, and charity.

So powerful was Augustine's vision that his utopia became the blueprint for medieval society in Europe. In the tradition that evolved from Augustine, the feudal system was divided into classes, with the clergy at the top, the military leaders below the clergy, and the peasants at the bottom of the pyramid. Its very strength, however, set the stage for the decline of feudal society. Class division came to be resented by those who, from generation to generation, were denied a share of the governance and the social goods such as wealth and power. The system was successful as long as each member of society accepted the role laid out in the class structure. When many peasants came to reject their state of intergenerational poverty, the feudal system was set for collapse. A tyranny of orthodoxy was present when the "right-minded" views of those at the top of the upright pyramid were imposed on the peasants at the bottom.

Augustine shared Plato's view that only the few were capable of turning the cards down. When those suited for leadership occupied the uppermost part of the upright social pyramid, order in the state was assured. Disorder, according to the Platonists, followed when persons not suited for leadership were placed at the top of the pyramid.

The Platonic-Augustinian model came in for serious challenge in the late Middle Ages. Aristotle had challenged Plato's conception of the just state, and during the eleventh and twelfth centuries an Aristotelian revival took place in Europe. The Aristotelian tradition as preserved and transformed by Jewish and Muslim thinkers made its way back into Europe through Spain. We turn now to examine the major impact the Aristotelian revival had on European thought as it addressed the tyranny of orthodoxy that arose with the Platonic-Augustinian school in the late Middle Ages. Also see Rosemary Radford Ruether's criticism of Augustine in Chapter Nine below.

The Aristotelian School: An Inverted Social Pyramid

Aristotle

Aristotle, who came from Macedonia, studied for twenty years under Plato in Athens. After this long period of apprenticeship, Aristotle turned on its head Plato's account of morality and the just state by inverting Plato's pyramid. He regarded the restrictions against marriage among the guardians to be too stringent. In a state having women and children in common, Aristotle argued, love will be watery. People love particular persons, according to Aristotle, and the love of humanity begins with the love of particular persons.

Aristotle also rejected Plato's foundation for justice—the theory of Forms. A world of nonphysical Forms that duplicates the world of particular physical things is too complicated, in Aristotle's view. He was aware that the debate between the dualists and the materialists had been going on for centuries, and he did not think Plato's solution to the controversy was satisfactory. Whether physical things or nonphysical things constituted the ultimate reality was a question that Aristotle did not think could be answered. He was a practical man of science, and he responded to the concern about ultimate reality with a suggestion that such an issue be approached by asking what we know for practical purposes.

Aristotle observed that it makes sense to accept the existence of minerals, plants, animals, and humans. It is also meaningful to ask about the relationships between these groups. If one is to be ranked higher than the others are, the ranking might be determined by the function or functions of each group. Plato had ranked humans higher on a scale of being by virtue of the access to special knowledge that humans possess. Knowledge of mathematics, geometry, and logic, Plato thought, distinguished humans from animals. When Plato gave his account of the source of this knowledge, however, Aristotle was not satisfied. Plato regarded knowledge of Forms, including those of mathematics, geometry, and logic, as innate. Such knowledge, according to Plato, gave humans access to knowledge of what ultimately is real. Humans could attain this knowledge through the exercise of speculative reason. Aristotle, on the other hand, held that knowledge of an ultimate reality may lie beyond the capacity of humans. Humans, however, can gain practical knowledge, and such knowledge comes through experience and practical reason.

Humans, Aristotle maintained, are not distinct from animals by virtue of innate knowledge. Rather, humans are distinct by virtue of the type of action that they can perform. Each group has its unique function, and that function includes the function of "lower" groups. When an individual attains the function typical of its species, it achieves what Aristotle called its "perfection." Minerals exist, while plants both exist and grow. Animals, in turn, exist, grow and move about. They possess locomotion, a function or perfection not possessed by plants. Animals also have the capacity for sensation. Humans have the functions of each of the other groups: they exist, grow, move about, and have sensation. In addition, however, humans have another function.

Aristotle used the term "reason" to describe the additional function. It is important to remember, however, that he rejected Plato's account of reason. So we must probe some to understand what Aristotle meant when he used that term.

Humans were unlike animals, according to Aristotle, since humans possessed the capacity to reason. Humans could attain more than mere pleasure and experience more than mere pain. Humans could aim at more than mere existence or the satisfaction of everyday wants. Humans could aim higher and try to attain a self-subsistent, good life—that is, a happy life. The good life was a life of self-sufficiency or self-subsistence, but humans were unable to become self-subsistent in isolation. Humans by nature, Aristotle maintained, are political animals or social beings. Humans can attain the self-sufficient, good life only in communities.

In communities or groups a natural division takes place for the purpose of governing. The soul naturally rules over the body, and the mind or rational element directs the body or passions. In the family or private domain, according to Aristotle, the male naturally directs the female. The governing of the state or public domain is ordinarily best performed by those who embody the rational element. The natural order of the rational element over the passional nature also explains why Greeks (Hellenes) govern barbarians: barbarians are generally governed by kings in isolated clans or tribes. Larger communities, in contrast to tribes and clans, tend toward greater self-subsistence. Greater self-subsistence, in Aristotle's account, was a sign of a more fully rational people.

The role of the state is to enable each person to attain the potential given by nature. Aristotle inverted Plato's social pyramid and said that the leaders play their appropriate roles when they assist people in attaining their potential.

Aristotle studied the governments of over one hundred different societies. While Plato proposed that rule by the few, or aristocracy, was the ideal form of government, Aristotle acknowledged that different forms of government—monarchy, aristocracy, or polity—may be suitable in different societies. He proposed that individual self-realization was the measure of the just state. When Aristotle left open the prospect that self-realization is attainable in a society ruled by the many (a polity), he planted a seed that was to come to full flower in some forms of moral liberalism—namely, the view that everyone is capable of turning the cards down and adopting the perspective of fair-mindedness.

Aristotle faces two main difficulties with his position—a tyranny of perfectionism and a problem with social stability. The tyranny of perfectionism can arise with the Aristotelian moral framework. The character of people is the primary focus of moral evaluation, according to Aristotle, and those lacking virtue may be described as morally deficient. The potentials of people vary according to their place on a chain of being. Disagreements over the human functions or the conceptions of the good life can divide communities. Since the potentials that people possess are so varied, conflict can arise over which functions or perfections to attain.

An inverted pyramid is unstable if one tries to set it on solid ground. Aristotle found his self-realization theory compatible with either rule by one, rule by the few, or rule by the many. While this view was quite tolerant of different systems, it lent itself to considerable division among later Aristotelians. Thomas Aquinas, for example, favored monarchy as the best form of government.

For further criticism of Aristotle's perfectionism, see the section on Lucius Outlaw in Chapter Five below. Also see Jean Bethke Elshtain's and Elizabeth Spelman's criticisms of Aristotle in Chapter Nine below.

Thomas Aquinas

Thomas Aquinas witnessed the early stages of the decline of feudal Europe. The demands of the English people for greater decision-making power were formalized in the Magna Charta in the decade prior to Aquinas' birth. The Christian crusades to win the lands of ancient Palestine from the Muslims had been waged during the preceding century. Aquinas, against the objections of his political family, withdrew to the Dominican monastery, where he gathered about himself texts from the Muslim, Jewish, as well as the Christian traditions. Although Aquinas remained closer to a moral communitarian, he produced a synthesis of thought in the *Summa Theologica* that laid the seeds for the reformation of Christianity and the rise of modern science.

Aquinas discovered in the Muslim (Averroes and Avicenna) and the Jewish (Maimonides) commentators on Aristotle extensive criticism of the Platonic system. Aquinas saw the power of the Aristotelian system to address some of the difficulties with Platonism, which through Augustine had come to dominate European thought and social structures.

Aquinas incorporated Aristotle's inverted pyramid, in which the leaders were viewed as primarily servants of the people who helped the people realize their potentials. Aquinas transformed Augustine's transcendent God into the notion of the good within each person. Each individual, according to Aquinas, had the potential for good as well as for harm. To attain one's natural function, however, was to seek the potential for the good within. This potential for good was a potential to discover a higher moral law that lies within each person. It was, to use the metaphor of the Rawls Game, the potential to turn the cards down on issues involving harmful relationships between humans.

Aquinas drew upon Augustine's list of virtues, but he re-interpreted the meaning of each of the virtues. Faith, for example, was taken by many followers of Augustine to mean a blind trust in a transcendent

God. For Aquinas, however, faith was closely associated with doubt. To have faith or to believe that something was true implied some doubt. A framework of doubt surrounded human knowledge, according to Aquinas, and this doubt reflected the limits of human knowledge. To claim to know more than is warranted, Aquinas held, is to overstep the bounds of human reason. A boundary or perimeter surrounds human knowledge. Claims to know a transcendent God or the will of God take one beyond that perimeter. Human existence, according to Aquinas, is surrounded by a sea of uncertainty. According to Aquinas, one attempted to discover one's purpose by attaining the potential given by heredity, environment, and self-awareness. The realization of this potential was sought within a community, not as an isolated individual.

The moral community, according to Aquinas, was not a particular community—Christian, Muslim, or Jewish. It was rather the human community itself. To attain one's potential was to attain one's unique function as a human being. The virtues were to be found, as they had been for Aristotle, within practices; virtues arose from and were specific to particular practices.

The problem of instability for the Aristotelian school is illustrated by Aquinas' preference for rule by one. Individual self-realization and social stability are best attained, Aquinas claimed, through a monarchy. The structure of society for the Aristotelians could take various forms—rule by one, the few or the many. The measure of justice was whether individuals could attain their potentials. As Aquinas' defense of monarchy illustrates, the variety of political structures permitted by the followers of Aristotle reduces the stability of society.

The cards are down to decide the good life in communitarian decision-making. Problems with the cards down include a tyranny of orthodoxy and a tyranny of perfectionism.

Strict communitarians, as we have seen, regard the social pyramid as upright, and moderate communitarians hold that it is inverted. An inverted pyramid implies that the leaders are the servants of the people, not their rulers or masters. Class division and the resentment that accompanies a caste system are problems for strict communitarianism, and the tyranny of perfectionism is the main problem for moderate communitarianism.

These problems with communitarianism have contributed to the emergence of modern liberalism. Some liberals, as we will see in Chapter Four, address the tyrannies of orthodoxy and perfectionism by leaving the cards up. Conflicts over who can turn the cards down and what it means to invert the cards can be avoided when the cards are left up. Other liberal philosophers place strict limits on what can be decided when the cards are turned down. Rawlsians will turn the cards down only for decisions on what is seriously harmful–e.g., slavery and religious intolerance. The cards will remain up for decisions concerning the good life.

In Chapters Six and Seven, we will see that some moral and political philosophers also attempt to stabilize the inverted pyramid by floating it in a sea of uncertainty that surrounds life. They do not attempt to place it on a solid foundation of claims about what is ultimately real and true

Chapter 3: Roots of Modern Moral Liberalism

Ancient and Medieval Roots

The modern human rights movement is a product of various influences in the history of ideas. The possessor of rights and the determiner of the good life in contemporary Western liberal democracies typically is the individual. The notion that the individual is the possessor of rights, however, was foreign to the main ancient and medieval communitarians. Similarly, the communitarians regarded as implausible the view that the individual was the main determiner of the good life.

Two major influences from the ancient world laid the seeds of modern moral liberalism. The schools of thought known as Epicureanism and Stoicism were advanced as philosophies of consolation for individuals. Meaning and purpose were unattainable through communities, according to Epicurus and Epictetus, so the individual was thrown upon his or her own resources to provide any meaning that life might have. The individual determined the kind of life worth living–that is, the good life. The Aristotelian revival of the late Middle Ages was also a major factor in the emergence of moral liberalism.

Epicurus

The Greek philosopher Epicurus was a founder of a type of hedonist philosophy. Epicurus' name is preserved for posterity in the philosophy of Epicureanism. According to Epicurus, the life worth living is a life of long-lasting pleasures. He advocated withdrawal from public life, where intrigue and conflict led only to individual unhappiness. People should surround themselves with a few close friends, withdraw to a private garden, and engage in a simple life and the pleasant conversation of philosophy. Longer lasting pleasures are preferable to immediate gratification, according to Epicurus, since they are conducive to more enduring and therefore greater pleasure. Similarly, passive pleasures (desire for food, sleep, friendship, and the absence of pain in the body and trouble in the mind) are preferable to active pleasures (desire for exotic foods, sexual pleasure, expensive clothes, fame and popularity) since they are more enduring.

Epicureanism was built on a foundation of certainty. According to Epicurus, knowledge gained through sensation is certain. To doubt sense knowledge, according to Epicurus, is skepticism. Epicurus accounts for error as a product of judgment, not sensation.

In answer to the question "What ultimately is real?" Epicurus accepted the atomism of Democritus. Critics challenged the atomist position. pointing out that something physical has dimension and that anything with dimension can be divided in half. The process of division, as described in the discussion of Democritus in Chapter Six below, can go on infinitely.

In response to the critics, Epicurus proposed that the smallest units were what he called "minima." Everything consisted of these ultimate minimal particles, which had shape, size and weight. They constantly bumped into each other. Smooth particles formed liquids and gases, and jagged particles formed solids.

Epicurus explained free will as a swerving of the atoms in motion. A complete determinism was impossible, according to Epicurus, since it reduced people completely to automata.

Epicurus presented an early version of a social contract. He regarded justice as nothing more than an agreement between people to abide by certain rules. These rules were chosen and revised as necessary to promote people's welfare.

Epicureanism was a philosophy of consolation. Epicurus advised people not to fear death or the gods. There is no more reason to fear one's non-existence after death, he maintained, than to regret our non-existence during the time before we were born. The study of physics does not support divine retribution. Hell, he maintained, is an illusion.

Critics of Epicureanism rejected it on the grounds that it reduced humans to mere pleasure-seeking animals.

Epictetus

In the Roman Empire, Stoicism flourished as a philosophy of consolation. Epictetus was a slave and guard to the Emperor Nero. Later he was freed and founded a school at Nicopolis in Epirus.

The rational individual determined the good and meaningful life in the thought of Epictetus. Epictetus regarded the individual as capable of appreciating the law of nature or world reason, which set down the fate of everyone and everything. Although every event happened in accordance with natural law, people were free in a very limited sense. Each could choose how to respond to events and could control his or her attitudes toward the inevitable working out of nature's laws. Resignation to the natural law was the highest virtue for Epictetus, an attitude that made life good and, to the greatest extent possible, meaningful.

Epictetus advocated that a main goal of education is to learn what one can and cannot control. One should then attempt to control only what one can. A person can control his or her will and attitude, so these should be the focus of one's reflections.

The Stoics held that humans have a natural capacity to distinguish good from evil. Evil comes from a perverse will, according to Epictetus. The pursuit of wealth is acceptable provided the wealth is used for a good end and one remains generous.

Epictetus opposed the Epicurean doctrine that the final end or goal of human life is pleasure. Humans, Epictetus argued, can pursue virtue. Among the virtues he advocated are truthfulness, loyalty, and performance of duty. Marriage and family are permitted, but those committed to the service of a larger community may remain celibate.

Moses Maimonides

Moses Maimonides was a twelfth-century Jewish philosopher who exercised a considerable influence in the twelfth-century Aristotelian revival. He was one of many authors who interpreted, preserved, and advanced the Aristotelian tradition. Maimonides attempted to reconcile reason and religion. In the Jewish tradition to which he belonged, this issue of reconciliation took the form of determining whether the 613 commandments of the Jewish Law were consistent with reason. One of his major works is *A Guide for the Perplexed*.

Maimonides represents a practical rather than a speculative orientation in philosophy. His concern with reconciling religion and reason may be taken as the question of whether faith is compatible with practical reason. This amounts to asking whether principles of action should be made with the cards up or the cards down. The perspective of faith is a timeless viewpoint represented by the metaphor of turning the cards down. The perspective of reason is long-term self-interest: people speak of individuals as rational when they protect their own survival and well-being as well as that of their loved ones. The main issue for Maimonides, then, may be expressed as the issue of whether a perspective of self-interest is compatible with a timeless perspective of fairness.

If rules are simply imposed, they do not assure fairness. While imposed rules may protect the interest to survive–at least in the short run–they do not insure fair treatment of individuals. Rules that are chosen by the people themselves, on the other hand, are more likely to protect fairness. Such rules are chosen from the timeless, cards-down perspective. If rules are reasonable they can be chosen by the people.

Maimonides provides examples in his *Guide for the Perplexed* of the fairness of specific rules. One rule that at first may seem irrational is that a heifer must be killed if a murder occurs and no one is arrested and tried for the murder. In his explanation of the rule, Maimonides points out that the murderer is more likely to be arrested when the rule is applied that requires a heifer to be killed. The heifer will in all likelihood be supplied by a local farmer. Since the locals often share information about crimes and since heifers are valuable to the farmers, the local who is asked to furnish the heifer may very well provide valuable information about the crime to the authorities. By increasing the chance of arresting a murderer, the rule may be taken as reasonable and be accepted by the people.

Transition to Modern Moral Liberalism

Thomas Hobbes

In the middle of the war-torn seventeenth century, the English philosopher Thomas Hobbes tried to make sense of the phenomenon known as morality. Religion, he was taught, was the foundation of morality. Yet when Hobbes looked around him, he saw civil wars fought in the name of religion. He turned to human nature rather than a divine nature as the source of morality.

When Hobbes observed human nature, he found that people by nature pursued self-interest. In a state of nature, he claimed, people have a right to anything they need or desire. Life, liberty, and property are sought to fulfill human needs, and for this reason anyone has a right to life, liberty, and property. The possession of these rights by individuals, however, leads to an endless conflict of rights–"a war of everyone against everyone."

Humans by nature are rather complex and clever creatures. To avoid perpetual warfare, according to Hobbes, humans enter a social contract with one another. Since each human is interested in the continuation of his or her own life and since people generally wish to live out their natural years, the majority agree to a government. The people can also agree to surrender most of their rights to the state. The benefit of transferring their rights to the state will, in Hobbes' account, be peace. Since humans follow the rule "Seek peace and pursue it," Hobbes argued, they enter the social contract. When a leader is put in place–whether the leader is a king who inherits the throne, a military leader who takes over by force, or an official who is elected by the people–a society moves from a state of nature to a state of civilization. To move to this state is to shift from the pursuit of immediate self-interest to the pursuit of long-term or enlightened self-interest. Hobbes regarded enlightened self-interest as the moral point of view.

The rights are transferred or "alienated" to the leader for the sake of peace. To keep peace, the leader must exercise absolute control over the people. Unless checked, people will pursue their self-interest; civil strife and warfare will result. Thus, the leader–or Leviathan, as Hobbes called the sovereign–must have complete power. It is the leader who possesses the rights; the individual citizens are subjects who live under threat of punishment for failure to follow the rules made by the leader.

Hobbes may be interpreted as holding that the cards cannot be turned down. Self-interest is the sole motivator for everyone, not merely for some members of society. Everyone "looks out for number one."

The inevitable conflict that arises with the cards up, according to Hobbes, may be managed only by an all-powerful leader who will make and enforce the laws. This leader is limited in the treatment of the people only by his or her own self-interest. Since the people would overthrow a brutal tyrant, it is in the interest of the leader not to engage in brutal policies.

Hobbes responds to the notion of natural law in earlier philosophers by describing a struggle to survive as the law of nature. The cards are up and people, either individually or in groups, struggle to survive and to engage in "commodious living." The vote to grant the Leviathan the right to govern is a majority vote. Some may vote against it, but in general people accept the contract.

Unlike his communitarian predecessors, Hobbes regarded the state as an aggregate of individuals. For the communitarians Plato, Aristotle, Augustine, and Aquinas, the state more closely resembled an organism than an aggregate. Injury to one member of the body politic was an injury to all; pain inflicted on one cell in the body was felt by all. Hobbes regarded each individual as separate from every other: each pursued his or her self-interest. Order could be kept only by an all-powerful leader.

With Hobbes, the shift away from divine nature and toward human nature as the basis of morality was set in motion for modern philosophy. Hobbes, however, held a rather pessimistic view of human nature. In the centuries since Hobbes, a number of accounts of morality have emerged that also look to human nature. Unlike Hobbes, however, most of these stories have a more optimistic view of human motivation. Also see the Carole Pateman's criticism of Hobbes in Chapter Nine below.

David Hume

David Hume, a Scottish philosopher, was one of a number of philosophers who, along with Hobbes, attempted to ground morality in human rather than divine nature. Hume's view of humans, however, was more optimistic than that of Hobbes. Hume held that humans are capable of sympathy for others, and the capacity for sympathy became in Hume's account the motive for morality. Hume proposed that the greatest pleasure for the greatest number is the standard of right action; what constituted the greatest net pleasure could vary from community to community.

Hume argues that an actual social contract was not the origin of government. Historically, people have accepted leaders who usurped positions of power or took over by fraud. They have not consented to leaders any more than children have consented to parents. Hume acknowledges that consent is the way things should be, the ideal basis for government. He does not, however, accept that societies in general have originated from a social contract. The Athenians and Achians came as close as any societies to governing by contract, but most of the people in these societies—the women, the children, the slaves, and the foreigners—were not consenting members.

Hume's account differed from those of the communitarians. Unlike the communitarians, who regarded society as an organism, Hume held that society consisted of an aggregate of individuals. The humans in the aggregate, however, had the capacity for sympathy—a capacity that Hume did not trace to a divine creator or to human reason. Hume and his followers in the utilitarian camp regarded sympathy as a product of human evolution. Darwin's later theories were consistent with Hume's account: environmental and hereditary influences explained the human capacity for sympathy. In humans, cooperative and altruistic behavior had survival value and thus evolved as a trait in humans.

Sympathy is the motive for morality, according to Hume, and morality can be traced to this capacity to feel compassion. If someone does not feel sympathy, Hume argued, we can explain why most people would not regard that person as a moral individual.

Sympathy for others provides the end or goal of morality. Reason serves this goal: it allows humans to discover the means to achieve the goals already set by the feelings. Because reason serves the feelings, Hume calls reason "the slave of the passions."

Chapter 4: Modern Moral Liberalism

Classical Moral Liberalism

The moral liberal regards the individual as the primary agent in moral decision-making. The community is not an organism; it is an aggregate of individuals. Liberalism rejects the common good of communitarianism and holds that an alleged "common good" is the sum of the individual notions of the good. Attempts to decipher the sum of individual notions of the good are needed to avoid anarchy. These attempts center on the protection of rights and the satisfaction of needs.

John Locke and Thomas Jefferson

As Hobbes before him, the English philosopher John Locke also attributed the emergence of a civil society to a social contract. Both distinguished between a state of nature and a state of civil society.

Locke maintained that people in the state of nature possessed rights to life, health, liberty, and property. The law of nature, according to Locke, was the law of reason. Individually the people in a state of nature enforced those rights. The state of civil society arose when the individuals entered a contract with one another to form one commonwealth and designate a representative body to enforce the rights.

The structure of an ideal state in Locke's proposal was the reverse of Plato's upright pyramid. Locke maintained that a state could not be just unless it consisted of a representative democracy. People who had no commonwealth to enforce the rights to life, liberty, and property remained in a state of nature. Groups of people such as native Americans who had no notion of private ownership of property remained in a state of nature. An absolute monarchy was also in the state of nature, according to Locke, since the monarch enjoyed the same liberties of private enforcement that individuals enjoyed in a state of nature.

Locke and his follower Thomas Jefferson, a Virginian who was the main author of the Declaration of Independence, provide the first major examples of moral liberalism's entry into the arena of public policy.

With Locke and Jefferson, the cards are down briefly as each individual chooses to enter the contract that forms the commonwealth. The unanimous vote of the citizens to form a commonwealth reflects the notion that rights belong to every individual. After the unanimous vote to accept majority rule, according to the Lockean proposal, the cards are returned to their face up position for policy decisions. As Ronald Green tried to illustrate in the first two rounds of the Rawls Game, people know their time and place when the cards are up. They know their abilities and their situation in society—wealthy or poor, advantaged or disadvantaged, and the like.

Locke and Jefferson rejected God's will and a divine right of kings as the basis for the state's legitimacy. The people were sovereign, according to Locke, and the government was legitimate when it upheld the natural rights to life, liberty, and property. Justice was satisfied when property was legitimately transferred, and a legitimate transfer took place when property was exchanged through income, inheritance, or gift. Theft was an injustice for the reason that it failed to respect the right to property.

Locke and Jefferson viewed rights as natural since, by nature, people have an interest in the valuable possessions of life and liberty. Locke added property to life and liberty, while Jefferson added pursuit of happiness. Although Locke included a right to health, it does not ordinarily appear in the list of basic rights possessed in the commonwealth. While Locke and Jefferson speak of the natural rights as God-given, they must not be mistaken for divine command theorists. They were proposing the alternative that the consent of the people rather than the will of God was the basis of the state's legitimacy. In medieval Christianity, the clergy was widely regarded as the main interpreter of the divine will. Jefferson attacks this function of the clergy and links it to "Platonisms" grafted onto Christianity.

The Lockean notion of justice may be called a retributive notion. The government in Locke's proposal could collect taxes to engage in those police functions that upheld rights: it could enforce laws against murder to protect the right to life, laws against fraud to protect the right to liberty, and laws against theft to protect the right to property. Beyond these, however, very few functions would be served by the government. The collection of taxes to redistribute the wealth was not a legitimate activity of the state. Redistribution for the sake of the poor and less well off would be taken care of through voluntary giving, according to Locke and Jefferson. Since taxes were not voluntary, redistributing wealth through taxation amounted to organized or state theft.

A major difficulty with the natural rights model may be called the tyranny of the powerful minority. Rights can conflict, and when they do some rights are typically overridden. The property rights of the wealthy during the industrial revolution frequently overrode the welfare rights–the right to life, for example–of the poor and the workers.

A second difficulty also arises when Locke turns to the majority vote. When a majority determines policy, a tyranny of the majority can occur in situations where the general welfare can be attained only by denying rights to a minority. When a majority vote, either by the people or their representatives, is the only acceptable procedure for policy decisions, the tyranny of the majority can take place. Also see the criticisms of Locke by Charles Taylor in Chapter Five and Lorenne Clark and Mary Lyndon Shanley in Chapter Nine below.

Thomas Jefferson and his descendants have personified the suffering over the issues of slavery and racial polarity that the U.S. has experienced during the past two centuries. While Jefferson advocated the abolition of slavery, he retained most of his own slaves. At the same time that he evidently fathered at least one child with his slave Sally Hemings, Jefferson did not think that social integration between whites and blacks was likely to occur. Jefferson was confronted with the censure of his white peers over the question of his having children with Sally Hemings. In his later years, the range of Jefferson's experiences was reflected in his statements on the issue of the social integration of Africans and Europeans. He wrote that the two groups could not come under the same government, so different were they in nature, habit, and opinion. He further stated: "The amalgamation of the one race [whites] with the other [blacks] produces a degradation to which no lover of his country, no lover of excellence in the human character, can innocently consent." See David Walker's response to Jefferson in Chapter Eight below.

Immanuel Kant

Immanuel Kant, a German philosopher, was one of the main figures of the eighteenth-century Enlightenment. Kant remarked that Hume awakened him from a dogmatic slumber. As Hume had done before him, Kant held that the individual determines the kind of life worth living, the good life. Kant, however, did not simply take the greatest pleasure of the greatest number as the measure of a right action. Kant probed for a perspective that would qualify as a universal moral point of view. When Kant gave his account of this point of view, he rejected Hobbesian self-interest as the measure. Inclination (toward fulfilling one's own interests or the interests of others) is not the motivation of morality. According to Kant, the choice of the rules by which humans govern themselves provides the motive of morality. Because we choose the rules, we are bound by the rules.

The standard of right action, in Kant's account, is what he called the categorical imperative. Kant expressed this standard in different versions. One major formulation is that an action is right only if it conforms to a generalizable principle. Another version of the categorical imperative is "Do not treat persons—either yourself or others —as means only but always as ends." A popular version of Kant's second formulation is "Don't use people."

Kantian thought is one type of deontologism. Deontologism regards an action as right if it conforms to a set of basic rules. In some forms of deontologism, these rules are divinely revealed, but in Kant's version the rules are the product of a social contract among humans.

The moral point of view that Kant aimed to express was not the point of view of self-interest, nor was it the altruist, utilitarian perspective. It was rather the fair-minded perspective represented in the Rawls Game when the cards are turned face down. The moral point of view, according to Kant, is the point of view of anyone. If a practice is accepted when the cards are down, it is a moral practice.

Persons capable of creating the rules by which humans govern themselves are deserving of respect. As such, each individual possesses rights. Rights, not needs—one's own or those of the greatest number—are the starting point of morality, according to Kant. Respect for the rights of each person is preserved when policies are negotiated with the cards down.

The utilitarians who came after Kant posed the question of whether keeping the cards down is the moral point of view. Such utilitarian thinkers as Jeremy Bentham, John Stuart Mill, and Harriet Taylor did not think such a viewpoint was possible. The cards are always up, they maintained, in the negotiation of the policies in human society. One could act out of sympathy for humanity, they contended, but the choice of the rules was not adequate as a motive for following the rules. Further, policies could be adopted unanimously that would not merit the label of a "moral practice." A practice of tying one's left shoe first, for example, could be adopted by anyone. Kant's point of view allows too much to provide an adequate description of an ordinary person's notion of a moral point of view.

The problem of a conflict of rights becomes the major problem for a Kantian position. This conflict can be illustrated with the struggles over the rights of owners and those of workers during the early period of industrialization. Exploitation of workers forced entire families–parents and children–into the mines and factories to earn enough money just to put food on the table. Children were deprived of education, and women were denied the opportunity to possess property or to vote.

When rights were invoked to justify public policy during the early industrial revolution and the period of chattel slavery, the property rights of owners were typically given priority over the welfare rights of workers. Reforms floundered as long as rights were the basis of appeal. The problem of a conflict of rights is illustrated by an even starker example. The brutal practice of chattel slavery allowed rights to the members of one group of humans but denied rights to another group of humans.

The utilitarian and socialist movements of the 19th century gave rise to the cry: "Needs first, not rights." When people's basic needs were not being met, Marx and others rejected rights as the foundation of a just society. When the basic needs of all are met, Marx asserted, the society is just.

Locke and Kant represent an early version of liberalism, but they do not reach the stage of classic liberalism carved out by the utilitarians. Locke and Kant resemble liberals in general in their claim that the individual determines the good life. They also share with other liberals the view that altruism or self-interest, or a combination of the two, may motivate the individuals' choices concerning the kind of life to lead and the meaning and purpose of life.

The liberalism of Locke and Kant differs from that of the utilitarians on the question of turning down the cards. While utilitarians keep the cards up for all policy decisions, Locke and Kant turn the cards down and adopt the cards-down, fair-minded perspective for some communal decisions. Locke and Kant differ over what may be decided unanimously with the cards down. Locke maintains that people can unanimously agree to accept majority rule, but Kant goes beyond Locke and holds that the morality of many actions can be determined from the fair-minded, cards-down perspective.

With the rights-based theories of Locke and Kant, we see a separation between public policy and the private sphere. Some criticisms of Kant have their origins in this division. Public law was a product of a social contract, according to Kant, while law in the private sphere was patriarchal, tribal, or religious in origin. Kant illustrated the public-private law difference by saying that the life of the villager is a life governed by public law, but the life of the nomad is governed by private law. Villagers had the capacity for democratic self-government, but nomads were capable only of tribal, patriarchal or religious law. Kant's criticism of some peoples reflected this preference for the way of life of an autonomous, enlightened villager. His characterization of medieval Christianity and Jewish religion as legalistic (see Chapter Eight below) and his dismissal of African idolatry reflected his preference for the democratic way of life based on social contract. For this reason, Kant's position was subject to collapse into a tyranny of orthodoxy, in which only some peoples were viewed as capable of turning down the cards. This criticism of the tyranny of orthodoxy is further elaborated in the section on the Kantian position of John Rawls below. For further criticisms of Kant, see Annette Baier's position in Chapter Five and the comments by Susan Mendus in Chapter Nine below.

In the next sections on the utilitarians Bentham, Mill, and Taylor we will see that the cards remain up for policy decisions. All decisions concerning what is right, good, and just are made in the utilitarian proposal with the cards up.

Jeremy Bentham

A reform movement was initiated during the early years of industrialization to address various problems posed by changing social conditions–including the widespread suffering of workers. Among the leaders of these reforms were philosophers known as utilitarians. Jeremy Bentham was prominent among the early English utilitarians.

Bentham sought to give greater weight to the voice of workers and the disfranchised. He popularized the notion that each should count for one and no one for more than one. By this Bentham meant that the basic needs of each individual were to be taken into account in policy decisions. The desires of the rich and powerful were to be given no greater weight than the needs of the poor and powerless.

Bentham challenged the notion of a social contract. In place of a consent-of-the-governed standard Bentham proposed that the standard of justice and morality be "the greatest pleasure of the greatest number of sentient beings." Policies that increased the sum of pleasure in the world were right; policies that produced more pain than pleasure were wrong. The shift to pleasure as the standard has won for the followers of Bentham the label "hedonist utilitarians."

Utilitarianism is one type of consequentialist moral theory. Consequentialism looks to the results or consequences to determine the rightness of an action.

"Natural rights are nonsense," Bentham wrote, "and imprescriptable [unalienable] rights are nonsense upon stilts." Bentham challenged the view of the contractarians that liberty rights (property and the various liberties) should take priority over welfare rights (life and the pursuit of happiness). When these two types of rights come into conflict, Bentham maintained, welfare rights should take priority.

Critics of Bentham's position claimed that Bentham had reduced human happiness to the level of animal pleasure. Mere pleasure was the standard of right action, according to the critics, and the quality of human life was indistinguishable from that of animals.

John Stuart Mill and Harriet Taylor

The utilitarian movement in 19th-century England accompanied the rise of socialism and was probably a major factor in the history of ideas that kept the Western democracies from going completely socialist. After Bentham, the main spokespersons for utilitarianism were Harriet Taylor and John Stuart Mill. The roots of utilitarianism may be found in the ancient philosophy of hedonism as expressed by the philosopher Epicurus.

These authors echoed Bentham's warning against adopting a fictional social contract as the framework of a just society. Sympathy for humanity, they proposed, was the motive for morality. Sympathy or devotion to individuals may be expressed, according to Mill and Taylor, but within the limits of the collective interests of humankind.

The standard of a just policy or right action, they maintained, was the greatest happiness of the greatest number. Mill and Taylor addressed problems left by the standard as formulated in the hedonist utilitarianism of Bentham—namely, the greatest pleasure for the greatest number.

Mill and Taylor distinguished between higher and lower pleasures and proposed that competent judges—those with the experience of both kinds of pleasure—prefer the higher pleasures. Unlike Marx, who made the greatest happiness of all the measure of a just state, the classical utilitarians Mill and Taylor offered a more workable, less utopian goal of the greatest happiness for the greatest number. The perspective of the impartial benevolent spectator is the moral point of view, according to the utilitarians.

As in Hume, compassion was the motivator and the end of life was fixed. Reason merely served the emotions in selecting the means to the fixed desires of an absence of pain and a general sense of well-being. Self-interest was taken into account, but the individual counted only as one among others, each of whom was given the same weight. As Hume before them, Mill and Taylor held that people were capable of sympathizing with the good of others.

Utilitarians regarded the efforts to ground public policy in rights as misdirected. Conflicts over rights became a source of widespread human suffering during the early years of the industrial revolution. Property rights of factory and mine owners were often given priority over the welfare rights of workers, and working families suffered the ravages of poor wages, inadequate housing, and a lack of education. The religious persecutions had driven many emigrants from Europe in the sixteenth and seventeenth centuries; in the nineteenth century, the industrial devastation of social Darwinism produced many more waves of immigrants searching for a new and better world.

In an effort to reform such harmful social situations, utilitarians make the claim that the right or just policy is the one that produces the greatest good of the greatest number. They try to bring back as a basis for public policy the notion of the good or the good life, but their attempt is distinctly different from the efforts of the ancient and medieval communitarians. The communitarians based policy on the notion of the common good: the policy that is most likely to promote the good of the community, viewed as a single organism, is the right or just policy. Utilitarians, by contrast, view society as an aggregate of individuals, and each individual determines for himself or herself the kind of life or lifestyle to follow. The "greatest good of the greatest number" is then the sum of the individual notions of the good life, not the good of the group viewed as a single organism. Utilitarians regard the right or just policy as that policy most likely to produce the greatest amount of good for individuals, with the good determined by the individuals themselves. The "common good" as conceived by the ancient and medieval communitarians disappears from the liberal notion of the good in utilitarianism.

Utilitarians are sometimes accused of subjective relativism, since the individual is the sole determiner of the good life. The classic utilitarians–Taylor and Mill–defend themselves from the charge of relativism with their claim that the motive in public policy decision-making is benevolence or altruism. Compassion for humanity is the motive of morality, and public policy can be placed on moral grounds when people act out of sympathy for humanity. Benevolence, according to the utilitarians, is the moral point of view. In utilitarianism, this perspective is what the utilitarians have in mind when they speak of the point of view of the impartial benevolent spectator.

Critics of utilitarianism have responded to the claim that benevolence or altruism is the moral perspective and have charged that some people are not benevolent. Hume replies to this charge by pointing out that persons who are not benevolent are commonly regarded as immoral. Mill and Taylor reply that, while most people may be self-interested, they recognize that benevolence is the motive of morality. The feeling of benevolence is present in most people, they maintain, and people regard themselves as moral when they express this feeling.

With benevolence as the motive of morality, utilitarians do not need to turn the cards down for policy decisions. The policy that is likely to produce the greatest good for the greatest number is the just policy, and no contract made with the cards down need enter the picture. Keeping the cards up allows the utilitarians to avoid the endless controversies and civil wars fought over the question of who can turn the cards down –that is, which individuals are capable of wise leadership or which societies are capable of civilized living.

Here lies the major difficulty for the utilitarians: if needs (welfare rights) are given priority over liberty rights, individuals can be used for the good of the greatest number. When the liberty rights of one individual or of a minority are overridden for the good of the majority, a form of tyranny sets in—namely, the tyranny of the majority. The protection of individual liberty rights becomes the major difficulty for utilitarians. Also see the criticisms by Alasdair MacIntyre and Charles Taylor in Chapter Five, G. E. Moore in Chapter Seven, and Mary Lyndon Shanley in Chapter Nine below.

Karl Marx

Marx was born in Germany but spent many years of his adult life in England. He joined a large group of 19th-century supporters of labor who were concerned about the shortcomings of natural rights as a basis for justice to workers. Marx proposed an alternative to natural rights. He kept the cards up, to use the metaphor of the Rawls Game, but he proposed that the needs of the many took precedence over natural rights. The use of the terms "needs" and "rights" is sometimes confusing among the utilitarians and Marxists. Some utilitarians, for example, claimed that welfare rights to life and pursuit of happiness took precedence over liberty rights, particularly the right to property. This is the same notion that Marxists or more moderate utilitarians generally have in mind when they say "Needs first, not rights."

Some commentators place Marxist socialism in a category different from liberalism. Equality is the overriding value in Marxism, however, and all persons are to receive equal shares of the social goods. For this reason, Marxism is classified as an extreme form of utilitarianism, a classification that explains why Marxism is often referred to as a branch of the "liberal left".

Marx's conception of justice, in contrast to Locke's retributive theory, is a distributive theory. The state's function, according to Marx, is to assure that the basic needs of all are satisfied; so for this purpose the state can engage in redistribution programs. The state is legitimate, he held, when it assured that the basic needs of all are met. Programs to assure the equal distribution of wealth, income, and other social goods are thus societal obligations.

A majority vote in the Rawls Game illustrates the Marxist and utilitarian support for the interests of the many. While utilitarians such as Mill and Taylor require that the state satisfy the greatest good of the majority, Marx's proposal that the state assure the basic needs of all are met is an extreme form of utilitarianism. To accomplish this extreme goal, Marx held, equal distribution of social goods is required. Altruism or benevolence provides the motive for action in Marx. Sympathy for the least well off, he held, could prompt state action to provide food and shelter to all.

In *The Communist Manifesto* Marx, with Friedrich Engels, claims that the shift from feudalism to capitalism has seen ownership of property transferred from the one to the few. One-tenth of the population, in Marx's estimate, control the wealth in capitalist societies, while the remainder of the people are made to work for subsistence or below-subsistence wages.

History, as Marx interprets it, has been a class struggle against ownership by the one or the few who exercise dominance over the many. The struggle will continue until the many take control of the property and the means of production. At such time, class division will wither away and the need for government will diminish. This will be the communist stage and will complete the struggle that began during the primitive period of human development, continued in the feudal period, and occurred in Marx's day in the capitalist stage. The proletariat (or class of workers) struggles in the socialist stage to wrestle ownership of capital and the means of production from the bourgeoisie (or capitalists).

Marx, in *Critique of the Gotha Program*, contends that since communism is evolving from a capitalist system, at first the arrangements will be "from each according to his ability, to each according to his contribution." Contribution will be measured by the quantity of work performed. Only later in the communist stage will the ideal be reached: "from each according to his ability, to each according to his need."

After Marx's death, Engels published Marx's work "The Origin of the Family, Private Property, and the State." The family began as a commune, according to Marx, in which each man and woman had multiple sexual partners. Children were raised in a communal arrangement. As society progressed from the savage, through the barbaric, to the civilized state, monogamy evolved. Marx considered monogamy the standard of male-female reproductive practice in civilized societies. Monogamy as practiced in capitalism, however, reduced the woman to a domestic servant.

The reduction of the woman to the status of servant occurred when the line of inheritance shifted from the mother to the father. Inheritance through the mother had developed in the savage and barbaric periods since the question of who was the actual mother of a child could be readily established with certainty. The emergence of nomadic and agricultural ways of life was accompanied by a system of patriarchy in the control of property. In this patriarchal system, the need to assure that only the actual genetic offspring of the father inherit the family's property led to severe prohibitions against infidelity on the part of the mother.

Only when the socialist state redistributed property, according to Marx, would the woman be liberated from her servitude. Monogamy would continue in the communist state, but as a matter of choice and not of coercion. Should affections change, separation of husband and wife could be more readily accomplished, since the complications of inheritance would be eliminated under the communist system.

Utilitarianism in all forms–including its Marxist form–can sometimes result in a tyranny of the majority. The liberty rights of individuals and minorities can be overridden to protect the needs, or welfare rights, of the many. An additional difficulty with Marxism is that equal distribution removes incentives. Marxism eliminates private ownership of the means of production. If personal gain is not available as an incentive, productivity falls off. In this instance, fewer social goods are available to distribute to the population. Also see the criticism of Heidi Hartmann and Jane Humphries in Chapter Nine below.

Contemporary Liberalism

John Rawls

John Rawls, who grew up in Baltimore, Maryland, offers a story of justice that attempts to eliminate some of the difficulties with previous social contract theories. He recognizes that many people have interpreted the social contract as an actual contract, and that some have also regarded the state of nature and the state of civilization as actual states occupied by identifiable peoples.

The difficulty faced by Rawls and other social contract theorists is how to stabilize an inverted social pyramid in which the leaders are viewed as servants of the people. An image that captures the proposal of some of the contractarians is that of a ship floating in the sea. A sea of uncertainty surrounds human existence, and speculative claims about what is ultimately real or true may overstep the bounds of human reason. Rawls defends his principles of justice without relying on an ultimate ground of certainty. These principles function in society much as a gyroscope functions to provide stability in a ship.

One source of difficulty with the social contract tradition is the identification of some people as living in a state of nature and others as living in a state of civilization. Such classifications have contributed to attitudes of colonialism and superiority of some people over others. Many members of societies who viewed their society as a state of civilization have regarded themselves as more advanced and enlightened than the groups they considered as living in a state of nature.

Rawls' correction of this attitude toward the members of some societies took the form of assigning to people in the state of nature the motive of fair-mindedness. In their natural state, according to Rawls, people are capable of turning down the cards. When they turn down the cards and negotiate the social contract, people negotiate the basic rights on which representative democracies are ordinarily built.

Once the rights are in place and the basic institutions are established to protect those rights, the cards are turned back up for legislative and other policy decisions in the state of civilization. Both altruism and self-interest may motivate people in the state of civilization; when excesses in the employment of either of these two motives lead to social division over the violation of basic rights–a division prompted when some people treat others in a tyrannical manner–the cards go back down for a re-negotiation of the basic rights. When these conditions arise, people employ the cards-down perspective of fair-mindedness to re-negotiate the basic rights.

In Rawls, the individual determines what kind of life is worth living, one's own lifestyle, and the meaning and purpose of life. Rawls, however, attempts to avoid a subjective relativist stance by accepting a minimum standard of human practices that is negotiated by the social contract. Slavery and other practices would be placed out of bounds, according to Rawls, because rational negotiators of the rules by which humans govern themselves would not accept such rules. They would not agree to the practice of slavery when the cards are turned down—that is, from the point of view of anyone, including the slave, who is the least well off in the society.

John Rawls makes a considerable effort to provide an account of justice that would apply to an industrial society. He attempts to retain the consent-of-the-governed standard from Kant and the equality standard from the utilitarians and Marxists. His effort to span the large chasm between capitalism and Marxism leads him to argue for the view that a welfare capitalist society is just.

His first step is to reject the natural rights of Locke as the foundation of the just state. Locke had maintained that a just state would protect the natural rights of life, liberty, and property. A state's failure to protect against murder, fraud, and theft provided grounds for the overthrow of the state.

Rawls regards no rights as given by nature. Rawls agrees with Kant that rights are negotiated or created by individuals from an impartial or moral point of view. The just state, according to Rawls, is a state that is built upon two principles. First, there should be maximum liberty compatible with an equal liberty for all. Secondly, inequalities in the distribution of goods are acceptable provided that they are to the advantage of the least well off and that equality of opportunity is available to all.

These two principles would be negotiated by those who enter the social contract behind what Rawls calls a "veil of ignorance." To negotiate from behind the veil of ignorance is to negotiate the rules with the cards down in the Rawls Game. Locke's notion of rights is equivalent to playing the game with the cards up and trying to reach unanimous agreement on specific policies. The unanimous agreement is required by the protection of each person's liberty. As illustrated in the Rawls Game, this Lockean approach can result in the tyranny of the minority. If, on the other hand, the negotiations were to proceed with the cards up and a majority vote were required to protect the greatest good of the greatest number, a tyranny of a majority could sometimes result. Rawls seeks to avoid both forms of arbitrary or tyrannical treatment of people by having the negotiators keep the cards down and negotiate from behind the veil of ignorance. He also refers to this impartial perspective as the original position.

Equality is present in Rawls' proposed principles. The first principle, which he calls the equality principle, requires equal liberty for everyone. The second principle, called the difference principle, includes the requirement that equality of opportunity be afforded to all.

Freedom is also present in Rawls' principles and takes precedence over considerations of social and economic needs. Rawls stipulates that the principle of equal liberty be given priority over redistribution undertaken to address social and economic needs. Rawls regards the virtues as secondary, but includes in his list of desirable traits fidelity, trust, justice, considerateness, fairness, and impartiality.

The Rawls Game illustrates Rawls' influential efforts to find a balance or a middle way between political factions on the left and right, between socialism and capitalism, between the liberal left and the religious right. The use of a game to understand Rawls is appropriate, since Rawls himself makes extensive use of game theory in his discussion of decision-making.

Rawls' position has some problems. Fair-mindedness includes Rawls' judicial virtues of impartiality and considerateness. Taken as the moral point of view, fair-mindedness would accurately describe a moral relationship between judge and defendant; it fails, however, to provide an accurate description of other moral relationships—such as that of parent and child.

The "perspective from eternity," or Rawls' cards-down perspective, can pose a major problem: it can deteriorate into a tyranny of orthodoxy. People may begin to argue over who is adopting the perspective and who is not. When people claim to adopt the perspective, they are sometimes subjected to proofs of fidelity and proofs of orthodoxy. Those unwilling to adopt the timeless perspective —and who prefer to follow inclinations, for example—may be viewed as infidels and on occasion may be subjected to inquisition and persecution. Battles can break out over who is orthodox and who is not.

The tyranny of orthodoxy can emerge in the following way. The turning down of the cards on such issues as slavery seems to be so right that anyone who is unwilling to invert the cards seems to be wrongheaded and lacking in fairness. The cards-down perspective, however, requires a willingness to suspend knowledge of one's place and time in the world. It requires the adoption of a timeless perspective. Some have called this an eternal perspective and have associated it with a religious point of view.

The tyranny of perfectionism, closely related to the tyranny of orthodoxy, is also a problem for Rawls. Philosophers in Aristotle's camp allow that, at least in some societies, everyone is capable of inverting the cards to determine the good life. The tyranny of perfectionism may occur in two ways. It can occur when a particular notion of what it means to be human is imposed on people who may not share that notion. It may also occur when a specific notion of the good life is imposed on some who have a different notion of the kind of life worth living. When Aristotelians maintain that everyone is capable of turning down the cards to determine the good life, they assume that everyone can agree on a conception of the good life. This turns out to be a highly questionable assumption.

Some of the main criticisms of Rawls have come from contemporary communitarians, including Annette Baier and Michael Sandel, whose positions are discussed in the next chapter. Also see the criticisms of Jean Grimshaw in Chapter Five below and that of Susan Moller Okin and in Chapter Nine.

Simone de Beauvoir and Jean-Paul Sartre

As representatives of another branch of contemporary liberalism, I have chosen two French authors who lived through the devastating wars of the first half of the twentieth century and whose writings were deeply influenced by the experience of those wars–Simone de Beauvoir and Jean-Paul Sartre.

A group of writers in Paris after the First World War was known as the "lost generation." After World War II, another group was labeled the "beat generation." In both cases, the name refers to a loss or a defeat. Both groups included philosophers who came to be known a existentialists. The starting point for existentialism was the view that humankind had lost a foundation for meaning. Religion as a public source of shared meaning that grounded public policy had collapsed some centuries earlier. A new scientific foundation had replaced the religious and was the source of great hope: science supposedly would dispel the superstitions and personal competitions that had led to arbitrary religious authority and endless civil wars. Science had been heralded as introducing a new day of technology, industrial cooperation, and international peace; public policy was now to be grounded in public rather than private beliefs.

Religion had provided a goal and meaning in life–namely, union with God in an afterlife. Science had substituted another source of meaning: better living through science in this world. With the earlier collapse of the religious foundation, both foundations–the religious and the scientific–were now gone when technology was turned to the cause of war rather than peace. Humans faced defeat in the search for a coherent account of the meaning of their existence. Each generation following these two wars in which technology was turned against people was "lost" or "beat."

In this setting, Simone de Beauvoir and Jean-Paul Sartre lived, thought, loved, and wrote. Beauvoir was a lifelong intimate friend of Sartre. Both of these writers saw in the grave injustices of the holocaust in World War II a complete collapse of moral responsibility. They traced this collapse to the loss of foundations for a meaningful existence. Life, they agreed, had become absurd.

In the philosophies of Edmund Husserl and Martin Heidegger, Beauvoir and Sartre found a clue for rebuilding meaning. Phenomenology, whose starting point is the analysis of consciousness, and existentialism were movements in the 19th and 20th centuries that became closely associated with the names of these four authors. Heidegger maintained that the awareness of death provided an occasion for humans to create their own meaning. Beauvoir and Sartre took this a step further. When an individual becomes aware that he or she will die, they held, that person is in a position to create meaning in life. Another existentialist writer, Albert Camus, put it this way: "The only serious philosophical issue is the question of suicide."

Many people have interpreted this starting point as pessimistic. The existentialists seem to be advocating suicide. Nothing, however, could be further from their intentions. Beauvoir and Sartre regard an attempted suicide as a form of inauthentic existence. "It is because man has something to lose," Beauvoir writes in *The Ethics of Ambiguity*, "and because he can lose that he can also win."

The notion of authentic existence is a central concept in the existentialism of Beauvoir and Sartre. To escape from the knowledge of one's death through a daily routine, blind belief in a religious or political doctrine, or living one's life through another person is to lead an inauthentic existence. A confrontation with one's own death is a condition of authentic existence.

Beauvoir describes her moral philosophy as an ethics of ambiguity. The human being is "ambiguous," since only in confronting meaninglessness can one find meaning. Only in confronting the fact of death, Beauvoir claims, can one attain freedom. The free life is the authentic life, and authenticity in the ethics of ambiguity is the only measure for evaluating a person. Authenticity is the only virtue. In *The Second Sex*, Beauvoir makes a compelling case that men have reduced women to the "other"–as minorities and colonized peoples have been reduced to the other by majorities and colonizers.

The existentialism of Beauvoir and Sartre has been criticized as providing a picture of an individual too isolated from others. In philosophy, an individual totally isolated from others in the search for meaning is known as a solipsistic individual. Beauvoir agrees that the individual whose source of meaning is his or her own death is isolated, but she does not agree that the individual in her philosophy is solipsistic. She sees the confrontation with one's own death as a condition of attaining the type of individualism advocated by Kant or upheld by the Christian ethics of salvation. Some remain unconvinced at her answer and see in the virtue of authentic individualism a potential for tyranny–a tyranny that echoes the tyranny of orthodoxy in religion.

Chapter 5: Modern Communitarianism

Twentieth-century communitarianism is represented in this chapter by authors who question various features of moral liberalism or develop communitarian theories. Alasdair MacIntyre, Michael Sandel, Charles Taylor and Benito Mussolini point to inadequacies with moral liberalism. Martin Luther King, Cornel West, Bill Lawson, and Lucius Outlaw raise the call from the African-American community for a fair racial game. Annette Baier, Sara Ruddick, and Jean Grimshaw give voice to injustices involving the treatment of women.

Critics of Moral Liberalism in the Anglo-American and European Traditions

Alasdair MacIntyre

Although the Scottish-born philosopher Alasdair MacIntyre refuses to accept the label "communitarian," he is regarded by many today as a foremost spokesperson for the movement in contemporary moral philosophy known by that name. MacIntyre accepts the label Aristotelian and attempts to identify several weaknesses of contemporary liberal moral philosophy.

MacIntyre challenges the account of a moral standard given by John Stuart Mill and Harriet Taylor. MacIntyre is concerned that their version of liberalism will collapse into relativism if it makes the individual the sole determiner of the good life. He speaks of the "privatization of good," by which MacIntyre means that the individual is the sole determiner of the good life. Utilitarianism, according to MacIntyre, completely separates the individual from the community, a separation that could lead to a Hobbesian war of everyone against everyone.

MacIntyre revises the utilitarian notion of "higher and lower pleasures" with a distinction between internal and external goods. He draws a distinction between goods external to and goods internal to a practice. Fame, power, and wealth are examples of external goods, while internal goods are the possession of skills specific to a particular practice and the pleasures that accompany the development of those skills. Thus, the internal goods can only be described in relation to particular practices. The internal goods are goods for the entire community of those who engage in a practice. The external goods are private possessions: the more that one receives the less there is available for others. Unlike liberal theorists who concern themselves primarily with external, quantifiable, and distributable goods, MacIntyre gives a central place to the internal goods and links internal goods with virtue. Virtues make possible the attainment of internal goods. The virtues of truthfulness, courage, and justice–among others– must be present if practices are to be sustained.

MacIntyre describes the teaching of the game of chess to a young child to illustrate how virtues arise from practices. Since the youngster is less interested in playing chess than in receiving candy, the teacher offers $.50 cents worth of candy if the child plays the game and $1.00 worth if the child wins. With candy as the goal, the child cheats and wins. MacIntyre comments that it makes sense for the child to cheat as long as the goal, candy, is external to the game. Goods internal to the game, however, cannot be attained through cheating. Skills specific to chess and the pleasures that accompany the knowledge of those skills are internal goods. To cheat is to deprive oneself of experiencing the goods internal to a game. It is to deny oneself the opportunity to know, for example, where one stands in relation to others who engage in the practice of chess. These conclusions about cheating are the products of the practical reason.

What is true of games, according to MacIntyre, is true of arts, sciences, the practice of making and sustaining a community, and the game of life itself. The ends of such practices and the internal goods that accompany them are not known in advance. Practices are rule-governed, but they involve more than mere rule-governed behavior. To engage in a practice is to exercise the capacity for practical reason; to exercise practical reason is to seek to discover the end(s) of the activities in which humans engage. These ends are not known in advance; the ends or purposes of human practices remain an open question in an Aristotelian approach.

As an Aristotelian, MacIntyre would hold that the cards can be turned down, following the metaphor of the Rawls Game, to determine the good life. Internal goods are pursued by those who engage in practices, and goods internal to practices are public goods for the practitioners. These public or shared goods are defined with the cards down. The common good, however, is defined only for those who engage in the practice.

A difficulty with MacIntyre's position is that it offers little or no help on the question of how to manage conflict in political societies. The good life is determined in communities, but these communities are smaller units than a nation-state. To claim that a common good can be found for a nation-state, MacIntyre maintains, is to invite totalitarianism.

MacIntyre responds to this difficulty with the claim that conflict is a permanent feature of human existence. Values, he holds, are discovered through conflict. This answer, however, leaves open the question of whether liberal nation-states should survive. The problem of the stability of the state, a problem we saw with Aristotle's model of the state, remains a problem in MacIntyre's account. Also see the criticism of Elizabeth Frazer and Nicola Lacey as well as that of Marilyn Friedman in Chapter Nine below.

Michael Sandel

The American philosopher Michael Sandel identifies a significant weakness in Rawls' liberalism. Sandel describes three conceptions of community. First, members of society regard the community as a means to achieve their own ends. This may be called the instrumental view of community in which individuals pursue self-interest. Secondly, members of society discover that others share sentiments of benevolence similar to their own. This Sandel calls the sentimental view of community. Thirdly, members of society conceive their identity as partly constituted by the community to which they belong. This view Sandel calls the constitutive view of the community. In the first two notions, the instrumental and the sentimental, the individual has an identity separate from and prior to any membership in community. In the third, no identity is possible or even conceivable separate from a community of which one is a part. Sandel defends the third view as the more plausible view of community. Rawls, according to Sandel, assumes a view of the individual held by those who subscribe to the instrumental and sentimental views of community—namely, the individual has an identity separate from and prior to any membership in community.

Charles Taylor

Charles Taylor, a Canadian philosopher, contrasts Kant's notion of freedom with 1) a notion of freedom commonly held among the ancients, and 2) a utilitarian notion. Unlike the notion of the ancients that freedom, in contrast with slavery, was a particular place in society and thus available only to some persons, Kant held that freedom was available to all persons. In contrast to the utilitarian notion that freedom was the absence of constraint on the satisfaction of desires, Kant held that freedom was consent to the rules by which humans govern themselves.

Humans, according to Taylor, attain their full stature as human beings when they formulate the rules by which they govern themselves. The utilitarian model does not allow the attainment of a unique humanity; the naturalistic underpinning of utilitarianism does not allow the ordinary person's perceptions of morality to be expressed. Among these perceptions is the view that some desires (or ends) are more fundamental than others. The end of acting out of duty (following the action chosen with the cards down) is higher than the end of acting from inclination (self-interest or altruism). Not just any natural desire satisfies the human being, but only those "higher" desires or ends that are sought—in the terms of our central metaphor—by unanimous agreement with the cards down.

Taylor defines "atomism" as the view that "men are self-sufficient outside of society." He associates this view with the social contract doctrines of Hobbes and Locke, and he considers whether rights can be based on an atomistic view of the person. He argues that atomism cannot support a doctrine of rights, and he rejects the view that rights so grounded constitute a foundation for political society.

An alternative, more plausible view of rights is that they make sense only within a social setting. He derives an obligation to belong to a community from an assertion of rights.

Benito Mussolini

Benito Mussolini helped to formulate the philosophy that shaped Fascism in Italy. He was head of the government in Italy between 1922 and 1943. His philosophy was an extreme form of communitarianism that claimed to address problems with other political philosophies. Mussolini criticized materialist philosophies and proposed that they be replaced with a spiritual philosophy. The state, he maintained, was both a spiritual and moral entity. The government was to serve as the conscience of the state.

Mussolini rejected both socialist and democratic forms of government. Socialism sought a final state of peace in which economic classes would disappear, but Mussolini countered that conflict was a perpetual state of human existence. Humans defined themselves as fit or unfit in the struggle for existence, both individually and collectively. The state showed its vitality in war and domination of other states.

Democracy was rejected as well. Mussolini regarded democracy as little more than a pretense of government by the people. He claimed that an invisible hand in the marketplace and hidden wielders of power actually do the governing.

True freedom, Mussolini argued, could be attained only when the state was viewed as the mind and soul of the people–a "corporative" state. The Fascist state that he defended was ruled by a few elite who embodied the mind and soul of the people. When the state was free, Mussolini alleged, the individuals were free as well. The state must direct the economy as well as the spiritual and moral life of the people. Only then would the state and the people truly be free.

Mussolini described the state as absolute and the individual as relative. He observed that the nation of Italy had not been a single state since the ancient Roman Empire, and he advocated the revival of the united Italian state.

Alasdair MacIntyre's observation that a communitarian philosophy can become tyrannical when applied at the level of the nation-state is confirmed in Mussolini's fascism. The aggressive Italian nationalism advocated in his extreme communitarianism met much opposition and contributed to the outbreak of World War II. Factions within Italy executed Mussolini in 1945.

African-American Philosophers

Martin Luther King

Martin Luther King grew up within sight of the state capitol in Atlanta, Georgia, where his grandfather and father were ministers at the Ebenezer Baptist Church. King experienced the indignity of legalized segregation and became a major leader in a non-violent movement to integrate schools and public places as well as to win equal voting rights for blacks. King studied philosophy and theology at Morehouse College and Boston University, and he drew on both the liberal and communitarian thinkers as he voiced opposition to segregation policies. From the liberal tradition he took the notion that individuals possessed rights and that rights require equal treatment of all. From communitarianism King drew the notions that the law of the state was subject to a higher moral law, an eternal law that is violated at a nation's peril.

With this powerful combination of sources, King's arguments became major factors in the civil rights movement that sought a fair racial game and an end to segregation. King argued that the segregation laws were unjust and found liberal and communitarian support for this contention. From the Thomistic tradition he drew the argument that segregation frustrated people in realizing their nature or potential. From the Augustinian tradition he presented the claim that segregation statutes failed to conform with a higher, eternal law. From the contractarian form of liberalism King developed the claim that persons subject to segregation and exclusion from voting were not given the opportunity to give their consent to policies. Armed with these arguments, King developed a major voice in the non-violent civil rights movement that brought an end to several overt forms of legal segregation in the U.S. during the 1960s.

Cornel West

Cornel West is a contemporary American philosopher who expresses some of the harsh reality and the hopes of African-Americans. West turns to the communitarian tradition for his framework and prescribes for the individual a conversion from meaninglessness and a sense of nothingness (nihilism) to a life of meaningful caring. The creation and preservation of social structures, built to prevent people from committing suicide, are goals that provide a source of meaning. The primary moral agent is the caring individual, whose virtues include service, sacrifice, love, care, discipline, and excellence. West draws on insights of Marx and attempts to integrate Marxist and communitarian thought.

West notes that calls for an end of philosophy are heard at several points in the history of ideas. Marx, Kierkegaard, and Nietzsche in the nineteenth century, and Wittgenstein, Heidegger, and Derrida in the twentieth century share the view that philosophy as a professional discipline or as a mode of thinking no longer serves as a source of meaning for individuals. Language about what is real is detached from the practical world of politics and power.

West traces the calls for philosophy's end to three sources: the view that science no longer provides an avenue to truth and reality, the questioning of authority in all forms, and a sense of impotence that leads to a deep despair concerning the future.

The retreat of philosophy from providing an account of truth and reality was gradual. It begins with Descartes. Modern philosophy was born with Descartes, who discovered a foundation for scientific knowledge in the individual's certainty concerning what is real. Since philosophy was the handmaid of science, the challenge to science as the authoritative voice on what is real and true–that is, the demythologizing of science–brought about the collapse of philosophy. The collapse occurred in several steps.

The first step was the reduction of the individual to a seat of experience by Locke, Berkeley, and Hume. Kant tried to restore the individual as the foundation of knowledge with his proposal that the individual's ways of understanding constituted the foundation of knowledge. Hegel equated Kant's ways of understanding with reality itself. Kierkegaard and Nietzsche recognized the threat to philosophy posed by Hegel, and they tried to return philosophy to its function of restoring and redeeming people. They detected no hope in the future in Hegel's philosophy: only the values and norms of groups, not those of individuals, mattered.

The roots of fascism and totalitarianism in the twentieth century can be traced to the collapse of philosophy and the loss of a place and an identity for the individual. Neo-Marxists (in particular, Stanley

Aronowitz and Herbert Marcuse) occasionally offer some glimpses of hope that reality and meaning can be restored for the individual. "Just as the Enlightenment era witnessed the slow replacement of the authority of the church with that of science, so we are witnessing a displacement of science, but there is no replacement as of yet."

The second source of the end of philosophy, the collapse of authority, occurs in both socialist and capitalist societies, but it is particularly pervasive in capitalist societies. Science keeps the citizens satisfied with new products, which are made attractive by clever advertising. Family, religious, and school authorities are placed second to the authority of the marketplace. West writes: "[T]he crisis of legitimacy–the undermining of the work ethic, the collapse of the family, anarchy in public schools, and the proliferation of sexually-oriented advertisements, commercials, movies, and television shows–becomes part and parcel of the very legitimizing processes of monopoly capitalist societies."

The third source of the end of philosophy–the sense of impotence–is prompted by ironic forms of thinking and narcissistic ways of living. The self-governing individual ("the transcendental subject") of Kant has been relegated in our day to a romantic notion of early capitalism; the Marxist collective as the source of hope has been reduced to a proletariat that remains "relatively dormant and muted." This desperate state of affairs is an ironic repetition of Hegel. West calls for a recovery of the revolutionary view of Hegel rather than an ironic repetition of Hegel. He finds the notions of negation and transformation in Hegel and Christianity to be the source of a renewal of society.

West sees in the work of Hegel, Marx, Kierkegaard, Nietzsche, and Foucault a recognition that words and concepts are rooted in a reality of power and politics. Afro-Americans can find in these writers a framework for their own prophetic and progressive traditions. A rich and diverse counter-discourse can be formulated to transform the racist discourse of modern European culture. With this effort, Afro-American philosophers can take their place alongside, not above, other committed Afro-Americans in the struggle for freedom.

Bill Lawson

The recognition that all humans–not just a few–are capable of fair-mindedness has already led many in the current generation of political philosophers to re-visit the notion of a state of nature. Bill Lawson, a contemporary African-American philosopher, has challenged thinkers who say that blacks have been and continue to be in a Lockean state of nature.

Lawson argues against those, such as Harvey Natanson, who contend that after the Civil War former slaves remained in a state of nature. Natanson maintains that former slaves could not have given their consent since the government did not provide the protection of the law during the period of Reconstruction. Further, Natanson holds that blacks were regarded as children and, in a paternalistic fashion, were given citizenship without the freedom to make the choice themselves. Natanson concludes that present-day blacks are in the state of nature and are not bound by the social contract.

Lawson replies to Natanson that blacks were not in a state of nature after emancipation, so blacks today are not in a state of nature. Many blacks consented to be citizens, and in this consent grounds were present for conscientious objections to groups who usurped political power on tyrannical, racist grounds. Citizens who are not given political protection do not cease to be citizens, according to Lawson; rather, they are citizens who have grounds for grievances against the government. If blacks today were in a state of nature, Lawson argues, they would be aliens. For this reason, their protests against tyranny on the part of the government would be acts of war against the government, not acts of civil disobedience. Lawson contends that the widespread agreement among blacks to be U.S. citizens makes them participants in the social contract.

Lucius Outlaw

Lucius Outlaw, an African-American philosopher, links a lower social status assigned to blacks in the U.S. to deep roots in the history of European ideas, including the ancient concept of a chain or ladder of being and the modern concepts of universalism and diversity. The view that some were higher and others were lower on a scale of being may be traced among European authors to Plato and Aristotle, according to Outlaw, and the influence of Plato and Aristotle during the European Middle Ages was extensive. Some people were regarded as higher or lower on the ladder of being, their position dependent on their abilities and behaviors. The arbitrary treatment that some people received when they were regarded as lower on a scale of being resulted from what was described in the section on Aristotle in Chapter Two above as a tyranny of perfectionism.

With this set of beliefs, Europeans were poised to relegate Africans to an inferior status during the Enlightenment and Romantic movements of more recent centuries. The need to classify persons according to race arose as contact increased among various peoples. When the slave trade emerged with the rise of capitalism, a need to justify the oppressive practice arose. Enlightenment thinkers employed a standard of rationality that they regarded as universal in defining qualities of humanness. The Enlightenment standard came to be regarded by the Romanticists of the nineteenth century as an imposition of a false uniform standard of humanness. To avoid an imposition of this sort, the Romanticists emphasized diversity rather than uniformity. For this reason, the descriptions of Africans–which, during the nineteenth century, were given under the guise of social sciences–emphasized diversity.

Although the Romanticists emphasized human diversity rather than universal reason in defining humanness, they did not avoid cultural expressions of racism. Diversity, in the tradition of the chain of being, had reflected the abundance and plenitude of the divine being. During the nineteenth century, diversity came to reflect more directly the romantic ideal of the unique value of each entity, including national and ethnic entities. The descriptions of racial differences, although well intended when set against the backdrop of the chain of being and Romanticism, tragically came to support racial divisions in the economic settings of slavery and segregation.

Outlaw takes Euro-American philosophy to task for its virtual silence on the injustice of the African holocaust. Many philosophers in the European traditions assumed a racial superiority of Europeans over others. Some–namely Kant, Hegel, Hume, and Jefferson–explicitly asserted such superiority.

He regards the search for unshifting foundations in philosophy as a contribution to imperialist projects. "At the very least," he maintains, "foundationalism...was a virtual accomplice to imperialist projects." Outlaw holds that African-American theorists generally have not come to terms with the realities of the social order in the U.S. and its blockage of the liberation of African Americans. Outlaw advocates a vision of a new society that would incorporate raciality and ethnicity.

Outlaw proposes that philosophy is best viewed as a product of a culture or the practice of a community and not as a transcendent, universal way of understanding the world. Communities have their own subject matters, texts, and practices. Schools of philosophy constitute different communities. One tendency of communities is to attribute contributions to the community's tradition exclusively to members of the community. European philosophy, for example, leaves out contributions of ancient Egyptians–the people of Kemet–to European philosophy. Such contributions should be included, Outlaw concludes, since the story of philosophy must addresses people of various races and ethnicities.

Feminist Philosophers

Annette Baier

The position of Annette Baier, who was born in New Zealand and has taught many years at the University of Pittsburgh, represents a contemporary form of moral communitarianism. Baier characterizes moral liberalism as a story that regards justice as the primary social virtue. She states that an adequate story of morality must include more than justice. Missing from the liberal accounts, she argues, is the care and sympathy for particular individuals as a motive for morality.

Morality begins in caring relationships, Baier maintains. Any story that fails to take this into account is simply inadequate. Baier finds in Hume's sympathy for particular others a central feature of morality; in addition, she finds in Carol Gilligan's account of women's approach to morality a story close to Hume's.

Baier criticizes Kant for tracing the motive of morality to choice of the rules. Unchosen relationships, Baier maintains, are the central feature of morality for women. At the center of morality is the care that accompanies unchosen relationships–for example, the love of a child for a parent in a relationship that the child did not choose.

Sara Ruddick

Sara Ruddick, an American philosopher, observes that women in white, Protestant, capitalist, patriarchal America have by-and-large stayed in the private, domestic realm. The public domain of government, business, and academe has not traditionally been accessible to women.

Ruddick suggests that the experience of women in the private domain has generated a maternal thinking that may be useful as women today enter the public domain in significant numbers. She finds a unity of thought and feeling that arises from the practice of nurturing, and she claims that maternal thinking is not more emotional or more relative to any particular reality (namely, the growing child) than the thinking that arises from scientific or religious practices.

The experience of mothering varies among cultures, but she expects some universal features of the experience may be identifiable. She expects that the perspectives of other cultures can translate her own perspective as she attempts to identify universal features of mothering.

Preserving, not acquiring, is a feature of mothering. Acquisition is associated with the technocratic society, but mothering is directed to the preservation of the life of the child. The competitive, hierarchical society poses a threat to a child; the mother recognizes and tries to protect the child from the dangers.

A virtue of mothering that stems from the mother's recognition of a child's fragility is clear-sighted cheerfulness. This attitude is present when one recognizes the harsh conditions that confront a child in the world but decides to nurture anyway.

In the face of practical uncertainties in protecting and nurturing a child, the virtue of humility is a requirement of mothering. Humility is to be distinguished from self-effacement; humility is sometimes equated with the self-effacement of subordinates in hierarchical societies.

Maternal thinking is not limited to biological mothers or even to females. Anyone may engage in the maternal activities of protecting the child, assisting its growth, and making the child acceptable to larger communities. While the protection of the individual child is a shared experience in mothering, the care may be directed toward anyone. In this respect, a central feature of the practice is universal.

Ruddick finds that the care-giving approach is an alternative to the objective, masculinist approach in academia. The alternative of care-giving also has political implications for militarist policies. Militarism runs contrary to the pacifism that is grounded in mothering.

Jean Grimshaw

Jean Grimshaw, a contemporary English philosopher, reviews various proposals that favor a female ethic and concludes that a separate female ethic may not be a successful answer to many contemporary ethical problems. She does accept, however, that the perspective of those who have nurtured children may make some difference in the kinds of public policies that may be adopted when women are policy makers.

Grimshaw traces efforts during the past few centuries to define a separate female ethic. Jean-Jacques Rousseau, she finds, describes female virtues associated with the simple rural life in which women played the roles of housewife and mother. Mary Wollstonecraft challenges the female virtues linked to these roles, citing the Victorian virtue of selflessness as an example of such virtues.

During the nineteenth century, Grimshaw recounts, female morality was sometimes thought to be superior to male morality. She traces this claim of superiority through twentieth-century thought and observes that, while the virtues of women in the nineteenth century were qualities desirable for domestic roles, female virtues during the latter part of the twentieth century have been regarded as qualities that could humanize the public sphere. Exploitative policies associated with war, politics, and capitalist economics have been traced by some feminist authors to male domination of the public arena.

Grimshaw considers whether male moral thinking is essentially different from female moral thought. Different accounts of morality presented by Lawrence Kohlberg, Carol Gilligan, and Nel Noddings have highlighted the issue of differences between male and female morality. Kohlberg finds that a morality of principles is the highest or genuine morality. Carol Gilligan finds that Kohlberg's description of morality–which echoes the positions of Kant, Rawls, and R. M. Hare–more accurately applies to males. Females, according to Gilligan, are drawn toward a morality that seeks to preserve relationships. Nel Noddings sees care as a central feature of female morality.

Grimshaw questions whether male and female thinking in regard to morality is as different as Gilligan and Noddings claim it is. She suggests that any differences between male and female approaches to morality could be explained as a difference in priorities: while men tend to value principles more highly, women favor the preservation of relationships. These different priorities stem from the different practices that males and females have ordinarily engaged in.

As practices in the industrial society have changed and women have more fully entered into the workplace, differences between male and female priorities have also broken down. The presence of females in what has traditionally been the public arena, an arena that includes the marketplace, has become more common. The shared experiences of males and females in the public arena make Grimshaw somewhat hesitant to accept generalizations based on sharp distinctions between male and female morality. Nevertheless, she accepts that the female practice of bearing and nurturing children is likely, as the presence of women is felt in the public arena, to bring about some change in present-day policies.

Part 2: Metaphysics and Epistemology

Chapter 6: Metaphysics

Metaphysics may be described as the study of what is real. The theme question of metaphysics is "On what grounds, if any, does it make sense to regard something as ultimately real?" Several answers have been offered, each apparently irreconcilable with the others. We will consider philosophers who represent five very different answers in the history of Western thought: materialism, idealism, dualism, teleologism, and humanism.

Democritus: Materialism

In answer to the theme question in metaphysics, "On what grounds, if any, does it make sense to regard something as ultimately real?" Democritus, an ancient Greek philosopher, proposes that materialist grounds provide the answer. He suggests that everything consists of the smallest physical particles, a view often referred to as atomism. His influence with this materialist answer is pervasive: his answer is accepted by Epicurus, Lucretius, Thomas Hobbes, Isaac Newton, John Dalton, Karl Marx, Harriet Taylor, and John Stuart Mill–among others.

The position of Democritus is influential because, at first glance, it appears to be straightforward common sense. If something is physical, it is made up of smaller physical units. Eventually it is composed of the smallest physical units. In answer to the question of what remains permanent through change, Democritus replies that matter is permanent. Change is explained as the result of the shift in the positions of the tiniest physical particles.

In Democritus' view, conflict is basic. No hierarchy or natural order is found. Any apparent order is explained as the random result of the bombardment of particles against each other.

Democritus' answer to the theme question, however, is rejected by Plato, Aristotle, Leibniz and a host of other philosophers, who maintain that looking for the smallest physical particles is in the same league as looking for square circles. They argue that the notion of a smallest physical particle is self-contradictory. Their reasoning is as follows. If "physical" means something with size or something that is measurable, Democritus' answer to the theme question is "Everything consists of the smallest things with size." Now if something has size, it plausibly can be thought of as further reducible in size–to one-half or one-quarter of its size. Democritus' answer now is equivalent to this statement: "Everything consists of the smallest things that can be further reduced in size." To look for such objects is akin to looking for square circles: we don't look for smallest physical particles because the notion is self-contradictory.

If Democritus' position is so readily criticized, its pervasive influence needs to be explained. The explanation seems to lie in this: Democritus' followers interpret him as saying that everything consists of the smallest functional physical particles. If people want to understand an automobile engine, they may take it apart and study its component parts. When the pistons, rings, camshaft and so forth are examined, they may be put back together to serve their functions when the engine runs.

Should people ask what a piston is made of and break the piston down into its alloys, they may gain an understanding of the components of the piston. Once the piston is broken down, however, it can no longer function in the engine. A piston is one of the smallest functional units in an engine; one gains an understanding of an engine by identifying a piston and understanding its function. To gain an understanding of the components of an engine, however, is not to gain an understanding of the ultimate composition of pistons. How an engine works is a question in engineering, but what everything is finally composed of is a question in philosophy.

Democritus is interpreted by many followers as claiming that everything is made up of the smallest functional physical particles, not the smallest ultimate physical particles. They interpret Democritus as offering an answer to a question in engineering or science, not as answering the question in metaphysics "On what grounds, if any, does it make sense to regard something as ultimately real?" From the failure of Democritus to answer this question, several schools arise, including idealism, dualism, teleologism, and humanism.

Pythagoras: Idealism

The ancient Pythagoras, who spent most of his life in the Greek city of Crotone in southern Italy, held that everything consists of the smallest units. These smallest units are either physical or nonphysical. It makes no sense, however, to regard these smallest units as physical particles: to do so is equivalent to looking for square circles. So these smallest units are nonphysical.

Numbers, in the numerical system used by Pythagoras, were represented by dots–as braille readers today uses dots to represent numbers and letters. Pythagoras regarded the dots used in representing numbers as ways of picturing actual numerical units. These units, he held, were quite real, but they were also nonphysical.

In answer to the question of what remains permanent through change, Pythagoras replies nonphysical numbers. The ultimately real units, according to Pythagoras, are nonphysical entities. His position is known as idealism. In holding this idealist view, Pythagoras reflects the notion that a basic harmony is present in the world, and this harmony is expressible in mathematical terms.

Parmenides: Idealism

The ancient Greek philosopher Parmenides adopted an unusual answer to the question of permanence and change. He joined Pythagoras in a defense of idealism. Parmenides denied the existence of change. His argument ran approximately as follows.

If something changes, it (the original thing) no longer exists. If something no longer exists, it has gone out of existence. But it is impossible for anything to go out of existence. Hence, nothing changes.

Parmenides responds to the question of what remains permanent through change by denying that change exists. Only the permanent exists.

Plato: Dualism

Plato found a middle ground between the extremes of the different answers offered by his predecessors to the question of what is real. He rejected the materialist answer of Democritus on the one hand and the idealist answers of Pythagoras and Parmenides on the other. Plato's position was known as dualism, the view that some things are physical and some are nonphysical. The position of Democritus was that the ultimate particles constantly bombarded one another and the world is fundamentally impersonal. To understand what was real, Democritus argued, each thing should be reduced to its component parts, and everything ultimately could be reduced to physical particles. Anything that could not be reduced to physical component parts, according to Democritus, simply did not exist.

In contrast to Democritus' view that everything is in conflict, Plato held that harmony is basic. The harmony of the universe was expressed in a hierarchical ordering of nature, according to Plato, and the harmony in nature mirrored a hierarchy in a higher, nonphysical world. Some things were higher and some lower on the scale of being, and their position on this scale was determined by whether they were closer to or further from the nonphysical Form of the Good. Things closer to the Form of the Good in the hierarchy possessed a more complete reality than those further away; those further from the Form of the Good had a less full existence or a less complete reality.

Plato found the idealist positions of Parmenides and Pythagoras to lie beyond common sense. Plato's middle ground proved to be a popular, common-sense position that resonated with many people for centuries and continues to find its adherents today. The twentieth-century philosopher Alfred North Whitehead commented that all European philosophy is a footnote to Plato.

Plato's answer to the question of what remains permanent through change is that non-physical Forms are permanent and material things change. A caterpillar, for example, assumes a different form when it changes—or is "transformed"—into a butterfly. The theory of the Forms may be better understood if you draw a circle and ask whether the figure you have drawn is a perfect circle. If you say that it is not, Plato asks how you know it isn't a perfect circle. Your answer could be that it is not perfectly round. Plato would observe that many people would agree with you and that in giving this answer you are comparing this to another, perfectly round, circle. He would then ask this question: As you compare the other, perfectly round, circle to the one you have drawn, where is the other circle located? If you were to say that it is in your head, Plato would then ask whether it is real or merely fictional. If you were to reply that it is merely fictional or imagined, Plato would then ask why so many people agree that the circle you have drawn is not perfect. Some notion of a perfect circle must exist, he would say, if we are to explain the widespread agreement that the circle on this page is imperfect. This notion, according to Plato, is the non-physical Form that we call a circle. The Form of the circle remains in existence and permanent, while particular physical circles–such as the one you have drawn–change or go out of existence.

The quest for knowledge of the eternal Forms provides a purpose for humans that sets them apart from other animals. Whereas animals are capable of pursuing only the pleasures of the senses, humans are capable of pursuing higher goods. Humans can attain knowledge of beauty (the arts), truth (the sciences), and goodness (moral philosophy). Knowledge of beauty, truth, and goodness will lead humans to produce beauty, tell the truth, and be moral. Knowledge of these higher realities, according to Plato, is the goal and purpose of life. When this purpose is shared and pursued by members of a society, the society can achieve internal harmony.

Aristotle: Teleologism

Aristotle parted paths with both Democritus and Plato. He regarded neither conflict nor harmony as basic in life. The debate over the issue of whether conflict or harmony was basic, Aristotle maintained, had not been settled despite centuries of dissension. Further, the issue was unlikely to be settled. Aristotle adopted another view. Conflict, he held, is part of life but people on occasion produce or discover harmony. The central issue is not to know whether conflict or harmony is fundamental, according to Aristotle, but to discover how to bring harmony from conflict–how, that is, to discover happiness and purpose in life.

In support of this purpose-oriented, or teleological, view, Aristotle first offers a response to the question of what remains permanent through change. Aristotle answers that form and matter are not things, but ways (or principles) of understanding: form is the principle of change and matter is the principle of permanence. He objects to overstepping the boundaries of human reason, and he sees the efforts of many of his predecessors as engaging in such overstepping. We may be unable to know what ultimately is real–matter or form. Rather than speculating on the unknown and perhaps unknowable, Aristotle focuses on what is known.

Aristotle's approach to understanding the world was a practical approach. He tried to grasp how things functioned rather than merely what they were made of. The term teleologism refers to this approach. As part of Aristotle's teleologism, he described four causes: material, formal, efficient, and final.

The material cause in Aristotle's account is what something is made of. The marble in a marble statue is the material cause. The formal cause is the form given to the marble. If the statue depicts a horse, the form is said to be that of a horse. The efficient cause is the maker or the sculptor of the statue. The final cause is the end or purpose served by the statue. It may, for example, be intended for use in a commemorative monument.

Humans, according to Aristotle, can and do know that minerals, plants, non-human animals, and humans exist. A reasonable question to ask is whether each of these has a specific function. Aristotle concludes that minerals, plants, and animals have their specific functions. Within the general categories of plants and animals, each species may be regarded as having species-typical functions.

All three types of things exist, but plants and animals have functions over and above those of minerals. Both plants and animals grow. Further, animals possess functions that plants lack: animals typically are able to move themselves about (they possess the function of locomotion), and animals are able to sense things around them.

Aristotle then comes to the question of whether the human animals possess a species-typical function. He decides they do: humans are capable of engaging in reason. They are aware that they will die, and this awareness gives them a capacity for sympathy and choice unavailable to non-human animals. The end or purpose of humans is linked to this unique function, according to Aristotle. Humans seek more than a life of mere pleasure, which is sought by all animals. Mere pleasure is an external good, and may be found in a variety of ways.

Humans seek a life of happiness, in which goods internal to practices may be pursued.

Aristotle challenges Plato on the issue of whether knowledge alone is sufficient to lead persons to pursue a more beautiful, harmonious life, to speak the truth, or to be moral. Aristotle holds that virtues are not attained through mere knowledge; the virtues, according to Aristotle, arise from practices. The modern Aristotelian Alasdair MacIntyre finds the pursuit of goods internal to such practices as games, arts, sciences, and making and sustaining a community to be the source of virtues. The development of the virtues in MacIntyre's account is described in Chapter Five. The purpose of the life quest, according to MacIntyre, is to discover the purpose of the quest.

Kant: Humanism

Kant rejected the views of both the dualists and materialists. Like Aristotle, Kant held that matter and form are not things, but ways of organizing experience. They are categories that people use to make sense of the flow of experience.

Kant, however, adds several items to Aristotle's matter and form. Kant holds that God, the immortal soul, the self, and freedom are not things; they are rather notions that people use to make sense of the world. He calls them "antinomies of reason." By this expression Kant means that cogent arguments can be given on both sides–for and against the existence of God, the self, and freedom.

The arguments over these issues have been going on for centuries, and Kant expects that they could continue for many centuries more. What are humans to do for morality and justice while these debates go on without any resolution?

We may observe that conflict is a feature of human life, but peace is also a feature of human life. At issue for Kant is how to create peace in the face of conflict. The way to peace is through justice, according to Kant, and justice is attained when people turn the cards down. The experience of freedom in human communities has been closely tied to the acceptance of rules made with the cards down. Unlike Aristotle, Kant does not base morality and freedom on a shared notion of the good life. For Kant, the only thing inherently good is the good will, and the good will for Kant is the will to turn the cards down and abide by rules made by unanimous consent with the cards down. Within the perimeters established by these rules, individuals are free to pursue their own notions of the good life.

Kant responds to the efforts to explain everything in physical terms. When people try to explain human behavior and beliefs completely in terms of heredity and environment, Kant points out, they leave out an important feature of human experience. While human behavior may be explainable in physical (biological or environmental) terms, such explanations address the human only from the perspective that humans may be studied as objects. These explanations fail to touch another perspective available to humans—namely, that humans are the subjects of their experience. From the perspective of a subject of action, Kant maintains, humans are radically free.

The pursuit of scientific knowledge was given a more substantial footing by Kant, as was knowledge of morality. Following Kant, we may say it makes sense to try to understand the function of small physical particles; likewise, to pursue knowledge of "the moral world within" is a legitimate enterprise. To claim that knowledge of matter, forms, God, and the immortal soul provides answers to the question of what is ultimately real, however, is to step beyond the limits of human reason.

In an effort to answer what ultimately is real, we have arrived at the question of the limits of human reason or human knowledge. Just what can humans know? And can they be certain about what they claim to know? These questions take us to another chapter in the history of ideas—epistemology or theory of knowledge.

Chapter 7: Epistemology

Two questions are closely connected in the study of epistemology, or theory of knowledge. The first we have already seen in metaphysics: On what grounds, if any, does it make sense to regard something as real? The second question is: On what grounds, if any, does it make sense to regard a belief (statement, proposition, and the like) as true? "What is real?" and "What is true?" are intertwined questions that underlie the various answers to moral, political, and religious questions.

Theories of Truth

The first issue that arises when one asks about the grounds for regarding a belief as true is the meaning of the word 'truth'. Three major answers have been given to this question.

Correspondence Theory of Truth

The answer to our question about the meaning of 'truth' seems at first to be quite straightforward: if my belief corresponds to an actual state of affairs in the world, my belief is true. If it is raining and I believe it is raining, my belief is true. If it is raining and I believe it is not, my belief is false. The correspondence theory holds that a belief is true if it corresponds with the facts. A belief is true, in other words, if what is in my mind corresponds with what is outside my mind.

This theory has a great deal of merit as a practical, everyday approach to truth. It gets into difficulty, however, when the frontiers of knowledge are involved. When differences of opinion over scientific and religious matters divide communities, what point of reference is one to use to decide what is the actual state of affairs outside the mind?

Pragmatic Theory of Truth

Another proposed answer to the meaning of truth is that a belief is true if it has good results. If it enables me to make accurate predictions, a belief is true. If it produces results that are beneficial to individuals, groups, or humanity at large, the belief is true. C. S. Peirce and John Dewey represent different versions of this theory.

The pragmatic theory of truth seems to support a scientific approach to questions of reality. The certainty that Peirce sought with the pragmatic theory in at least some of his writings may be called a scientism or a physicism. In its scientistic form found in Peirce, pragmatism offers a method that permits a correspondence between belief and fact; for this reason, Peirce's version is close to a correspondence theory. It seems to assume an orderly progress in knowledge, as hypotheses are confirmed or disconfirmed. Science, according to some critics, does not appear to progress in an orderly fashion. Thomas Kuhn describes movement in science as the result of paradigm shifts rather than progress in knowing what is real.

John Dewey described a practical notion of truth that stopped short of Peirce's claims. Rather than using scientific method to arrive at a knowledge of reality, as Peirce had proposed, Dewey regarded the practical goal of an increase in human welfare as the main project of science.

Coherence Theory of Truth

The coherence theory of truth is the view that my belief is true if it coheres with my other beliefs. The coherence theory is intended as an alternative to the correspondence theory, which requires an independent reality to confirm the truth of a statement. Francis H. Bradley, Brand Blanshard, Bernard Bosanquet and Otto Neurath represent coherentism.

One source of controversy among coherence theorists is the level of coherence required for a belief to count as true. At the most stringent level, all of a person's beliefs would entail the others. This level, however, is quite unattainable. A lower level of coherence is present when not all of one's beliefs entail the others. The level of coherence required for truth remains a problem with the coherence theory.

Knowledge: Theories of Justification

Several possible answers may be given to the theme question "On what grounds, if any, does it make sense to regard a belief as true?" First, a skeptical answer is a possibility. There may be no grounds or the grounds may be uncertain. The skeptical answer may be thought of as an infinite series of beliefs, none of which clearly provides a starting point for the rest. Secondly, a self-evident or irrefutable basis is also a possibility. From this starting point, a person could infer the remaining beliefs that he or she holds. This position is known as foundationalism. Thirdly, a person might base the various beliefs she or he holds on an initial belief, but this initial belief would not be regarded as irrefutably true. This position is called contextualism. Finally, a person could accept "coherence grounds"–that is, a belief is true if it coheres with the rest of one's beliefs. This position is commonly referred to as coherentism.

To make some headway in evaluating this range of possible answers, we may consider the purpose of our thinking about the grounds for true beliefs. Are we trying to find a way to express an accurate picture or representation of the world, or are we trying to find a way to deal with the world? Are we trying to find a way to hold a mirror to the world or are we trying to manage or cope with problems that arise in the world? The answer that we give to the representation vs. coping (problem-management) issue sets the stage for the foundational and non-foundational positions we will encounter.

Materialists and dualists have won the minds and hearts of people at different times in the history of ideas. When the stories of morality, law, society, and nature told by materialists and dualists reflected the stories that people in the street told, each school of thought received widespread approval. When natural explainers were prevalent, materialism rose to the fore; when supernatural explainers were more common, dualism won the day.

A way of expressing a harmony between morality, law, society, and nature is to say that a moral force has seemed to favor humans and make their lives more pleasant. Life became more pleasant in many respects when the agricultural way of life came to replace the nomadic. Dante's *Divine Comedy* represents a good literary example of a match between the moral and natural worlds in the agricultural society of medieval Europe. The physical cosmos and the moral world reflected each other. The various orders of being in the physical world, as Dante related in his story, matched the orders of being in the moral world. Platonic dualism, as developed by Augustine, expressed the harmony between the moral, social, and natural worlds.

Fate or nature seemed to favor humans in another transitional event in more recent centuries. When industrialization replaced the agricultural way of life and life became easier still for some people, material progress again seemed to occur. Nature's favoring of humans seemed again to provide evidence of moral progress. Materialism in the modern era came to be regarded by many as a better way to explain both the natural and moral worlds.

In general, dualism and materialism reflected two distinctly different conceptions of moral progress. Platonic dualists for the most part viewed civilization as a deterioration from an earlier, simpler world in which life had been better. War was increased by civilization. Moral progress could occur only if people retained the virtues of simplicity associated with the earlier way of life. Materialists, on the other hand, saw civilization as more peaceful than the barbaric earlier state in which humans had lived. Civilization, according to the materialists, decreased the incidence of war in the world. Moral progress could be made if people got rid of their barbaric ways.

In the nineteenth century, the cooperation of industrial and commercial enterprises was heralded by materialists—both Marxists and utilitarians—as a new day of cooperation that would replace the centuries of civil wars fought in the name of religion. If the primitive and patriarchal ways of the past could be discarded, according to the materialists, peace could be attained. This view was regarded as an optimistic view of civilization, and it was considered preferable to the pessimism of the Platonic worldview. Science came to replace religion as the avenue to human peace and well-being. Andrew Carnegie expressed one version of this new vision. The social Darwinist gospel of Herbert Spencer, he wrote, would replace a waning Christianity. Scientific progress rather than a pilgrim's progress was the way to increase human welfare.

Platonic dualists, by contrast, advocated a simpler life as the means to peace and harmony. They traced wars to excessive appetites for the consumption of goods. If a people consumed more than their society's resources could support, the Platonists held, eventually they would invade their neighbors' lands to acquire more resources. The Platonists called for less consumption and less greediness.

Dualism became a dominant model for agricultural societies. The virtues of temperance, courage, and wisdom advocated by dualists provided a sensible way of assuring justice in society. When these virtues were followed, war could be avoided. Materialism, on the other hand, became a dominant model for industrial societies. The cooperation made possible by transportation and commerce could replace the competition among neighboring peoples for resources. The new forms of civilization made possible by industrialization could bring about a new day of unprecedented peace and cooperation in the world. Walt Whitman in the nineteenth century wrote that he could hear America singing this new song of material progress.

The certainty that accompanied the match between the natural and moral worlds in the medieval world of feudalism gave way to a new certainty during the period of industrialization. A match between morality and science replaced the earlier medieval harmony between morality and religion. The dream of a better world beyond one's death gave way to the Marxist and utilitarian dream of a better life for the present and future generations in this world.

The dream of freedom from uncompensated or under-compensated labor (slavery or wage-slavery) was fueled by the vision of the industrial revolution. The vision was so clear and so readily understandable that vast millions came to share it. If the workers of the world could unite, Marx argued, a new utopia of an equal share for all could be attained.

An undercurrent of opposition to the foundational views of materialism and dualism has been present throughout the history of ideas. The tendency to claim certainty for a particular world-view—materialist or dualist—has been resisted by thinkers in every generation. Among the more recent voices is that of the African-American thinker Lucius Outlaw. As mentioned above in Chapter Five, Outlaw regards the search for unshifting foundations in philosophy as a contribution ("a virtual accomplice") to imperialist projects.

Radical Foundationalism

Foundationalism is the view that a person's set of beliefs is grounded in factual or self-evident knowledge. A two-tiered structure of knowledge operates in this way of understanding knowledge. The first tier is the foundation—as in a house or pyramid—and the other tiers are built on the first and consist of claims or beliefs inferred from the first tier.

An argument that has been used indirectly to support foundationalism is the infinite regress argument. Beliefs can be thought of as links in a chain. A chain may either be infinitely long or it may have a starting point. Foundationalists have defended the alternative that a chain of beliefs must start somewhere, arguing that an infinitely long chain of beliefs is inconceivable and results in epistemological relativism. Radical foundationalists maintain that the starting point of the chain must be a first principle or principles known to be true.

Classical or radical foundationalism is represented mainly by the thought of the French philosopher Rene Descartes. Thomas Hobbes and John Locke may also be described as foundationalists. Hobbes speaks of knowledge of fact as absolute knowledge, which he contrasts with knowledge of consequences. The knowledge of consequences is a conditional knowledge associated with science. As Descartes had done before him, John Locke viewed the mind as a mirror to nature: knowledge is accurate if the representation is accurate. The mind is a blank slate, a *tabula rasa*, according to Locke, and knowledge is present when the mind accurately mirrors the external reality. In more recent times, the representationalism or logical atomism of Bertrand Russell is a form of foundationalism.

In the history of ideas, rationalism and empiricism have been closely aligned with foundationalism. Among the rationalist philosophers we have studied, two efforts to arrive at certainty in regard to truth have been foundationalist. Augustine developed what may be called theologism and Descartes adopted a position that could be described as mathematicism. Theologism will be examined under philosophy of religion.

Descartes' mathematicism attempted to find the same type of certainty in morality and religion that he found in mathematics. He thought that certainty could be found if he could build his account of reality on a self-evident truth. Such a self-evident truth (or axiom) he claimed to have discovered in his famous *cogito, ergo sum*: "I think; therefore, I am." He arrived at this basic certainty after doubting everything–the existence of God, the immortal soul, the world around him, and even his own existence. When he doubted his own existence, he finally overcame the uncertainty. He could be sure, he concluded, of this much: in order to doubt, there has to be a doubter.

Descartes eventually overcame his skepticism. His approach has been described as methodic doubt. This means that his doubt provided a method to overcome uncertainty. His position did not conclude that nothing could be known–which would be a complete skepticism. His position turned out to be skeptical in method only–hence its name "methodic doubt."

After proving his own existence, Descartes then faced the problem of proving the existence of the external world. He proceeded to do so by logical deduction, beginning with the certainty of his own conscious existence. After establishing with certainty his own existence, he then claimed to prove the existence of God by arguing that as a perfect being God must exist. If a perfect being did not exist, Descartes argued, that being would be lacking existence and thus would not be perfect. Criticisms of this argument will be presented in Chapter Eight below.

With the existence of God established to his satisfaction, Descartes addressed the question of the existence of the external world. The external world, according to Descartes, included all physical things. His own body was among the physical objects of the external world.

Descartes' proof for the existence of the external world appealed to the notion of a clear and distinct idea. If he had a clear and distinct idea that a physical object existed, he reasoned, a perfect being would not deceive him in such a belief. He regarded the idea of his body as a clear and distinct idea, and he concluded that God, a perfect being, would not deceive him into believing that his body existed if in fact it did not. With this conclusion, Descartes completed his application of the method of logic or mathematics to attain certainty on the issue of what sorts of things exist. This method, as Etienne Gilson points out, may be described as Descartes' mathematicism.

Descartes faced the difficulty that the self as he conceived it was divided into two separate entities–mind and body. The separation of mind and body became an insurmountable problem for Descartes' theory. He tried to overcome this separation by proposing a causal interaction theory that the mind caused events in the body, and the body caused events in the mind.

Descartes' causal interaction theory failed when the question was raised: How can a nonphysical entity cause physical events to take place? Physical things–let's say the balls on a billiard table–are located in space and time. The event that causes an effect precedes the effect in time. The movement of one billiard ball, for example, causes the movement of a second when the two make contact. The movement of the first ball precedes the movement of the second ball in time, and the first makes contact with the second ball in space.

The event (the movement of the first ball) that causes an effect (the movement of the second ball) precedes the effect in time, and the cause (the first ball) makes physical contact with the effect (the second ball) in space. A nonphysical thing is located neither in space nor time, so it is unclear how it can make contact or precede physical things that are located in space and time.

Within the rationalist and empiricist schools, however, critics warned against overstepping the bounds of human reason and linking too closely the questions of what is true and what is real. Their warnings were sometimes prompted by the realization that too close a tie between the questions of reality and truth could give an illusion of certainty on other important matters–namely, what is good, right and just, and on the question of whether God exists.

The Emergence of Anti-foundationalism

Within each of the four traditions we are about to examine–the Aristotelian tradition, German idealism, American pragmatism, and the analytic tradition–a shift has occurred from foundationalism to anti-foundationalism. Some positions in each of the schools are foundationalist while other positions within the schools illustrate the move toward non-foundationalism or anti-foundationalism. This movement has been particularly noticeable during the nineteenth and twentieth centuries.

The Aristotelian Tradition

Aristotle. Aristotle adopted a more moderate form of foundationalism than did Descartes. Aristotle held that first principles grounded practical knowledge. Tom Rockmore points out that in Aristotle, first principles, such as the law of the excluded middle, must be assumed if any discussion is to take place. An example of a statement that illustrates the law of the excluded middle is "something cannot be and not be at the same time and in the same respect." Statements of this sort must be accepted as true, according to Aristotle, before any meaningful discussion can take place between people. In the practical realm of action one's purpose—or final cause, in Aristotle's language—was the first principle.

Alasdair MacIntyre. MacIntyre has described human practices as activities surrounded with uncertainty: he includes in his description of human practices the notion that humans don't know why they engage in arts, sciences, making and sustaining communities, and games—including the game of life itself. The uncertainty felt by humans as they engage in practices, according to MacIntyre, is an enduring feature of human existence. Within human practices, people act without the certainty that radical foundationalists seek.

German Idealism

Immanuel Kant. Kant also took a more moderate position than did Descartes on the question of the foundations of knowledge. Kant describes his own position as a Copernican Revolution in philosophy. Copernicus had revolutionized popular understanding of the relationship between the earth and the sun when he claimed that the earth circled the sun. His view gradually won acceptance and replaced a geocentric view—the view that the earth is the center of the universe and the heavenly bodies circle the earth.

People sought to discover a permanent external reality outside their minds. Kant rejected the notion that the mind was a blank slate, a passive mirror to an external reality. Kant proposed that both the mind and the external reality contributed something to the act of knowing. The mind contributed categories through which the flow of experience was interpreted. The external reality presented data, such as one event regularly followed by another event. The mind, however, contributed the category of cause and effect. The flow of experience was ordered by the categories, and a sequence of events could be interpreted as an instance of cause and effect. In one way Kant's view was antifoundational: a permanent, fixed reality remained outside the limits of reason. In another way, his view was foundational: the categories of the mind themselves became the ultimate reality–a view that Kant's followers developed.

Non-foundationalism claims that knowledge is possible without foundations. The non-foundationalist (or anti-foundationalist) positions have generally aimed to serve as correctives to arbitrary claims of foundationalists. Foundationalist claims at times have supported arbitrary uses of authority associated with the alleged certainties of dualism and materialism. Arbitrary religious authority grew out of the false certainties associated with established religion. Arbitrary scientific authority, in similar fashion, arose from the alleged certainties of scientific and pseudo-scientific claims.

The main type of non-foundationalism has come to be known as coherentism. A coherentist's answer to the justification of knowledge is quite different from the answer of the foundationalist. Foundationalists, as described above, claim that beliefs are based on a bed-rock foundation of factual or self-evident truths. A coherentist, by contrast, holds that to count as knowledge a belief must cohere with one's other beliefs.

Ernest Sosa has used the metaphor of a raft and a pyramid to contrast coherentism and foundationalism. The pyramid requires solid ground to remain upright, but a raft can float provided the logs that make it up are properly bound together.

The image of a chain has also been used to illustrate the contrast between foundationalism and coherentism. The chain of beliefs for the coherentist is joined at the ends and forms an endless loop. The chain holds together provided each of the beliefs coheres with the other beliefs. A foundationalist position claims that the first link in a chain must be solidly fastened to a bedrock, foundational truth or truths. The other beliefs are then grounded or supported by the foundational truth or truths.

Coherentism may collapse into a form of skepticism or relativism. The series of beliefs returns to the initial belief but then continues, as it were, in a circle. The circular process could go on infinitely. As long as a person looks exclusively within a system of beliefs the danger of skepticism or relativism persists.

G. W. F. Hegel. Hegel, a German philosopher, tried to answer objections to coherentism. His position may be classified as anti-foundationalist. Tom Rockmore offers the following account of Hegel's theory of knowledge. Hegel challenged an argument that dates back to Aristotle. Aristotle had claimed that a circular chain of beliefs could not ground knowledge, a criticism that remained the accepted view for many centuries. The linear chain of beliefs defended by Aristotle has been a traditional image to express the notion of a foundation of knowledge. To be grounded adequately, according to Aristotle, the first link must be a principle or principles known to be true. The grounding belief or claim must be factual or self-evident.

Hegel challenged the assumption that a chain of beliefs must be linear and foundational. A self-evident claim, Hegel argued, is not required to ground knowledge. He defended the antifoundationalist alternative that a chain of beliefs could be circular.

Knowledge can follow from a circular process, according to Hegel. The center point of a circle is not fully a center point until the circle is completed. The completed circle, he maintained, has a center point that can sustain knowledge.

Rockmore draws out some implications of Hegel's position. It is antifoundationalist for the same reasons, as we will see in the next section, that pragmatism is antifoundationalist: the truth of a belief in both Hegel and the pragmatists is determined by the consequences of the belief. Such an approach, Rockmore notes, collapses as a basis for knowledge. Knowledge that follows from a circular process does not provide the certainty ordinarily regarded as necessary for full knowledge.

The danger that anti-foundationalism may collapse into relativism or skepticism extends to other areas as well—morality (moral philosophy), justice (political philosophy), reality (metaphysics), and knowledge (epistemology). At the societal level, the central issue is whether people can accept a non-foundationalist view without also threatening the stability of their society.

American Pragmatism

C. S. Peirce. Although the general goal of the American school of pragmatism has been the non-foundationalist project to deal with the world rather than to provide a picture of reality, C. S. Peirce at some points uses the language of foundationalism. Peirce has been interpreted as an advocate of the view that if a belief allows accurate predictions about things in the world, the belief is a groundwork or foundation of knowledge upon which to build other beliefs.

John Dewey. Dewey, an American philosopher who is known outside of philosophy mainly for his educational reforms, tends to avoid the strong language of foundationalism; rather, he speaks of warranted assumptions that ground beliefs in particular contexts. Although he did not use the term "contextualism" to describe his theory, John Dewey provides an example of a school of thought known as contextualism.

Dewey tries to address the shortcomings of radical foundationalism with his contention that beliefs can function as foundational claims in different contexts. He rejects the representation of reality as a legitimate project for philosophy and proposes instead that philosophy's proper role is to employ experimental or scientific method to manage individual and social problems. Philosophy's traditional quest for certain knowledge of a fixed reality, Dewey argues, must give way to security and control in managing our lives. This control can be sought despite the continual changes that humans encounter in a dynamic world.

People have different interests in dealing with the world. These interests affect the way they view events in the world. An object, according to Dewey, is an event with meaning. A writer, for example, might view a piece of paper as something to write on. A scientist might view it as a collection of chemicals or atomic particles. The different views stem from the different interests that the writer and the scientist have in the piece of paper. These interests provide the context in which they address problems in living. The writer may use the paper as a means to convey her ideas or make a living or both; the scientist employed by a paper manufacturer may approach the paper as an item that can be improved upon. The writer who cannot find a piece of paper to write on may be satisfied when finally she discovers a piece.

For her, the statement "I now have a piece of paper to write on" may be basic in dealing with her surroundings in her present context. For the scientist, on the other hand, the statement "the chemical composition of this paper is such and such" may be basic. In Dewey's view, then, different statements or beliefs are basic in different contexts.

To count as knowledge, according to Dewey, beliefs must also be coherent. While the coherentists such as Neurath hold that a belief must cohere with one's other beliefs if it is to count as knowledge, Dewey maintained that a belief must cohere with one's practical experience. A belief that coheres with one's experience is a reasonable belief. The measure of reasonableness is whether a belief allows one to manage or direct the objects in one's environment. If one's belief enables the individual to manage problems and increase well-being, the belief then counts as knowledge.

In the first chapter of *The Quest for Certainty*, Dewey contends that the philosophical quest for certainty in understanding an immutable reality (God, Platonic Forms) has given way to a scientific quest for material security in life. He proposes that science may bring order and control from the disorder and chaos of the world. The realm of science is a practical realm and can provide a purpose, direction, and meaning in life. Rather than seeking psychological certainty in futile efforts to know what is real in a speculative realm, people can work toward material security in the practical realm and protect themselves from the ravages of nature.

Dewey writes that in the tradition certainty and security could be attained only in the realm of knowledge. The realm of action was one of uncertainty. "Through thought...it has seemed that men might escape from the perils of uncertainty." Security, according to the tradition, could be achieved only by adjusting one's inner attitude to destiny. With the emergence of the cooperative activities of science and industry, however, security from the vagaries of nature has become possible.

"Barring the fears which war leaves in its train," Dewey contends, "it is perhaps a safe speculation that if contemporary western man were completely deprived of all the old beliefs about knowledge and actions, he would assume, with a fair degree of confidence, that it lies within his power to achieve a reasonable degree of security in life." Dewey lists some of the ravages of nature from which humans seek refuge. He writes: "The precarious crises of birth, puberty, illness, death, war, famine, plague, the uncertainties of the hunt, the vicissitudes of climate and the great seasonal changes, kept imagination occupied with the uncertain."

In the final chapter of *The Quest for Certainty*, Dewey describes knowledge as inadequate for giving access to the real (the permanent or immutable). Yet he finds a place for scientific knowledge in providing meaning and order. He rejects the claim of many philosophers that knowledge provides access to the real in favor of the claim that a pragmatic, scientific approach provides knowledge of what is true. Truth as understood by the pragmatist, according to Dewey, is the source of meaning in the practical realm of action.

Dewey's position was formulated in the United States during the last part of the nineteenth and early part of the twentieth century. Present in Dewey's view is an optimism that reflects a confidence in science shared by many during this era. Science was to free humans from the bondage of nature and the superstitions of religion. Science, according to this view, was expected to increase the adaptation of the environment to human interests and to eliminate wars fought in the name of religion.

The confidence in science apparent in Dewey's writings has largely been eroded in the second half of the twentieth century. Environmental insults from the attempts to adapt the environment to human desires have contributed to this mistrust of science. Eugenic wars against minorities, undertaken in the name of science allegedly to improve humanity at large, have further contributed to this mistrust.

Dewey has expressed the thoughts of many that practical rather than speculative knowledge is the proper role of philosophy. At the same time, Dewey's writings provide an illustration of the weaknesses of this project. His optimistic expectations from science remind us that it is important to balance an optimistic and a pessimistic view of humans and their activities. His work also acts as a further reminder that neither religion nor science in itself is the guaranteed means to human betterment. Finally, it invites further exploration of the link between practical and speculative reason as people search for plausible moral and epistemological points of view.

The Analytic Tradition

G. E. Moore. Moore, an English philosopher, was one of the founders of modern analytic philosophy. He shared with Bertrand Russell a foundationalist theory that came to be known as a reference theory of meaning. They shared the conviction that ordinary language has a logical order that reflects a logical order of the world.

In his *Principia Ethica*, G. E. Moore examines the principles that ground the field of ethics. The province of ethics, according to Moore, is the whole truth about what is peculiar and common to ethical judgments. To approach such truth he proposes to undertake a general inquiry into what is good. In contrast to normative ethics, which seeks a universal norm or standard of right action, Moore's approach is described as metaethics.

The reference theory of meaning guides Moore in his metaethical undertaking. He states his goal as an attempt to re-think the underlying principles of ethics. The reference theory of meaning leads Moore to try to identify what the ordinary person has in mind when he or she describes something as good. Moore claims that people know what good means, although the meaning of good may not be definable. Just as a sighted person knows what the color yellow means but may not be able to define it, so people ordinarily know what 'good' means but are not able to define it. Moore claims that the meaning of good is a unique non-natural property known through intuition. This notion of good, in Moore's account, serves as a foundation for practical knowledge.

Moore shares with other analytic thinkers the hope that a clarification of terms used in philosophy will resolve traditional philosophical problems. Moore directs his attention to the question of what is good in an effort to address some of the traditional confusion he has detected and expose what he has seen as the "naturalistic fallacy." Moore makes his claim that 'good' cannot be defined after unsuccessfully seeking a definition of good that "describes the real nature of the object or notion denoted by the word." Past confusions have been related to attempts to define the term. He cites the work of Bentham and Mill along with several other philosophers as examples of this fallacy.

Moore analyzes the position of J. S. Mill and finds the naturalistic fallacy present. Mill has argued that pleasure is desirable because pleasure is desired. Mill's assumption in this argument, in Moore's analysis, is that what is desired is desirable. Mill attempted to defend the assumption by drawing an analogy between the word desirable and such words as visible. Moore replies that the analogy is false–that the better analogy would have been with words such as damnable and detestable ("ought to be detested," "deserving to be damned"). But the failure to perceive the false nature of the analogy allowed Mill to commit the naturalistic fallacy.

Moore's rejection of Mill's and other forms of the naturalistic fallacy hinges on a crucial argument against any attempt to define or analyze good. This argument begins with Moore's alternatives: either 'good' is simple, or it is complex, or it means nothing at all. He proceeds to show that 'good' is simple by arguing that it is neither complex nor meaningless.

Both alternatives involve a form of questioning. Moore rejects the assertion that good is meaningless by appealing to the common sense nature of the meaning of such questions as "This is pleasant, but is it good?" That the two terms are not taken as meaning the same thing is evidence for Moore that 'good' is not meaningless.

Moore's analysis reflects the reference theory of meaning. In keeping with Russell's theory of logical atomism, Moore regards things as divisible into their simplest parts. This simple, unlike the complex, is unanalyzable, indefinable, and can only be pointed to with an "ostensive definition." Moore's reference theory of meaning is apparent in his analysis of the good into its component simples. Moore held that the simple, unique, indefinable properties of 'good' were aesthetic enjoyments and personal affection.

Moore's view came under attack from one of its earlier proponents, Ludwig Wittgenstein, who argued in his later career against Moore's assumption in *Principia Ethica* that good can be determined by inspection to be indefinable.

A. J. Ayer. Ayer, an English philosopher, is also a foundationalist in the analytic tradition. He may be regarded as a representative for the philosophical position called "emotivism." His theory of meaning differs from G. E. Moore's in its focus on sentences rather than words.

Ayer acknowledges his debt to Russell, Wittgenstein, Schlick, and Carnap and places himself in the empiricist tradition of Berkeley and Hume. From Hume Ayer derives the distinction between "relations of ideas" and "matters of fact." Corresponding to "relations of ideas" in

Ayer's terminology is the *a priori* statement that is necessary and certain because it is analytic. Analytic statements tell us nothing about the empirical world, according to Ayer. Corresponding to "matters of fact" are empirical or synthetic statements, expressed as hypotheses the truth of which is probable. Ayer claims through the distinction and application of the verifiability principle to have provided an explanation of the nature of truth. Empirical statements that satisfy Ayer's principle of verification provide a foundation for knowledge.

The principle of verification, as presented by Ayer, states simply that a statement is meaningful if and only if it can be empirically verified–that is, verified through observation. Thus Ayer claims that any assertions about a world of values, the immortality of the soul, and the existence of God are nonsense statements or pseudo-statements. Philosophical statements are analytic, and the role of philosophers is to examine the language used in science to determine its logical relations and the meaning of the symbols. Ayer asserts that there should be no "schools" of philosophy, and he claims that his empiricist foundationalism has allowed him to give a definitive position on the traditional problems of philosophy.

From these grounds Ayer develops an interpretation of moral judgments. He poses the question: "Are ethical judgments genuine synthetic propositions?" Ayer gives a negative answer, which he arrives at in the following manner. He distinguishes several uses of moral language–definition of ethical terms (moral philosophy), the phenomena of moral discourse (sociology and psychology), moral exhortations (ejaculations and commands), and actual ethical judgments. It is primarily with the last that Ayer is concerned.

Ayer limits his question to normative ethical judgments, which he distinguishes from descriptive ethical judgments. In descriptive ethical judgments, the statement "x is wrong" means that x is commonly regarded as wrong. But Ayer asks whether normative ethical judgments can be reduced to non-ethical terms–that is, to genuine synthetic propositions. He notes three attempts to do so: subjectivism, utilitarianism, and intuitionism. He rejects subjectivism on the grounds that person A saying "x is wrong" and B saying "x is not wrong" would not be contradictory in the subjectivist's account. Each speaker, according to the subjectivist, is merely expressing a proposition about his own state of mind, and both could be true.

Ayer rejects utilitarianism on similar grounds. He finds it would not be contradictory to say that "It is right to do x, since it will produce the greatest good for the greatest number" and "sometimes it is not right to do x, even though x would produce the greatest good for the greatest number." Common usage is Ayer's basis for saying these are not contradictory.

Ayer's rejection of the intuitionist's position is based on the premise that there is no criterion for deciding against conflicting intuitions. In the absence of criteria, no evaluations are possible.

Since ethical judgments do not count as knowledge, no foundation for such judgments is necessary. Ayer finds the distinguishing feature of value judgments to be the same as that of imperatives–the emotive element. Because value judgments are expressed logically as imperatives, they have a lower logical status than indicatives: they are non-factual and thus cannot qualify as genuine synthetic statements. The function of value judgments is rather to express or evince feelings. According to Ayer, this is a process distinct from the subjectivist's account: the subjectivist had claimed the value judgment expresses a proposition about the speaker's state of mind, but Ayer denies that the value judgment is a proposition. The statement "It is wrong," he claims, adds nothing factual to the statement "You stole the money." Finally, in the function of expressing and evoking feelings, value judgments also influence behavior.

These tenets of Ayer are challenged by R. M. Hare. Hare believes the emotive function is a symptom–and an unreliable one–of value judgments: it is not the distinguishing feature. Hare also finds that imperatives do not merely express the wishes of the speaker. One would not, he points out, hire a detective to discover the reliability of a mayor's order by observing the mayor's expression. And Hare rejects the claim that the function of imperatives is to influence behavior. Hare finds the imperative to be an answer to the question posed by a rational agent, "What shall I do?" It is the function of propaganda rather than imperatives, Hare contends, to influence behavior.

Ludwig Wittgenstein. Wittgenstein was born in Austria and studied philosophy at Cambridge in England. During his early career Wittgenstein accepted the foundationalist theory of Bertrand Russell; he later moved toward an anti-foundationalist position.

The early Wittgenstein shared the enthusiasm of Russell, his mentor, at the possibilities posed by mathematical logic. During these early years his goal was to account for the whole of mathematics with the language of logic. At this time Wittgenstein shared with Moore and Russell the conviction that language followed a logical structure that reflected a logical order in the world.

Wittgenstein was eventually to abandon his confidence that a logical order in the world could be revealed through the analysis of language. Consistent with this position, Wittgenstein gave up the teaching of philosophy for a period of years. After serving as a soldier and being taken as a prisoner of war during World War I, Wittgenstein spent about a decade engaged in pursuits other than the teaching of philosophy. During this time, he built a house for his sister and taught elementary school.

In his later thought, Wittgenstein came to hold that different human practices give rise to different languages with various structures. One such human practice is mathematics. Wittgenstein introduced the expression "language game" to reflect this change in his position. Mathematics, Wittgenstein maintained, consists of many language games, and the meaning of these games consists of the uses to which the formulas are put.

Wittgenstein came to view philosophy as a therapy rather than as a way to gain knowledge of reality. He held, however, that the world determines the language games that can be played; for this reason, the selection of one's language games is not merely arbitrary. Language games, he maintained in his later career, are like the riverbed through which thought flows.

Wittgenstein provides a model for philosophers to be self-critical in their philosophizing and not to take their speculations about truth and reality too seriously. His expression "language game" suggests an element of play.

Part 3: Philosophy of Religion

Chapter 8: Arguments for the Existence of God

Rene Descartes

The foundationalist Descartes seeks certainty for his belief in God and claims to find such certainty in a proof from the history of ideas. This proof has come to be known as the ontological proof. Descartes tries to support a theistic view with his radical foundationalism.

Descartes lived in France during the seventeenth century, a time when science mounted many new challenges to the religious beliefs of the late Middle Ages. Galileo, an astronomer, was placed under house arrest after his conviction in a church trial for heresy in his scientific teachings. In this climate of thought, Descartes asked himself whether there was any room for value in a world of scientific fact. He was looking for a way to preserve the personal and the moral in an impersonal world of scientific fact.

Descartes regarded religion as the source of morality, and he tried to find a place for both religion and science. As we saw in Chapter Seven, Descartes first arrived at the certainty that at least one thing exists–namely, his conscious mind. Having established the existence of his own mind, he next entertains the notion of a perfect being and asks whether such a being actually exists. Some of the characteristics of this perfect being are father, creator, judge, all-knowing, all-loving, all-powerful, all-just, transcendent, incorruptible, eternal, and infinite.

Descartes draws on the eleventh-century philosopher Anselm for the ontological proof. The proof is very simple in form. It may be stated in this way: If a being is perfect, that being necessarily exists; God is a perfect being; thus, God necessarily exists. He defends the first statement or premise by saying that, if something were perfect but did not exist, it would lack something that even the simplest and lowliest being possesses–existence. A being could not be perfect if it lacked existence. In defense of the second premise he points to the characteristics of God listed in the previous paragraph–all-knowing, transcendent, and so forth–God is a perfect being. Descartes concludes that such a being exists and claims to arrive at this conclusion with certainty.

Kant rejects the ontological argument, charging that Descartes' proof is a "miserable tautology." By this he means that the argument is true by definition, but definitional truths (such as truths in logic and mathematics) may tell us nothing about what exists in the world. Kant tells us that some statements are true by definition and some are true by observation. The statement "All bachelors are unmarried men" is true by definition. We might claim in response that this statement is true by observation, since we observe bachelors as well as unmarried men and eventually come to realize that the two groups are the same.

To see the distinction between statements true by definition and statements true by observation, the following approach may be taken. A person could ask how he establishes the truth or falsity of the statement "All bachelors are (financially) rich." A survey of the financial status of bachelors–that is, an observation of bachelors– would be the appropriate way to establish the truth of the statement.

One could then ask whether a survey of bachelors is needed to determine whether the statement "All bachelors are unmarried men" is true. To learn that someone is a bachelor is also to learn that he is unmarried. To learn, however, that someone is a bachelor is not also to learn that he is rich. The notion of 'unmarried man' is already contained in the notion of 'bachelor', but the notion of 'rich' is not already contained in the notion of 'bachelor'. If one notion is already contained in another notion, the statement is true by definition; otherwise, when two separate notions are correctly linked, the statement is true by observation.

Charles Hartshorne maintains that Kant is incorrect when Kant says that observation is the only way to establish what is real. Hartshorne notes that the statement "All squares are circles" is false by definition. Hartshorne then asks us to think about this question: When was the last time you looked for a square circle? Since we do not go around looking for square circles, Hartshorne reminds us, we assume that our definitions (of squares and circles) tell us something about the real world–or at least we expect that they do.

Thus, the ontological proof for God's existence should read as follows: the statement "If a being is perfect, that being necessarily exists" is true by definition; the statement "God is a perfect being" is true by definition; therefore, the statement "God necessarily exists" is true by definition.

Whether the conclusion so stated tells us anything about an existing state of affairs is where the question stands. Do definitions define things or do they define words? Cartesians (followers of Descartes) have assumed they define things; others, including the humanist Kant, point out that they define words. We are left with these questions from the examination of the philosophy of religion: Do our words tell us anything about the ultimate nature of things? Are they limited to reporting what is observed? Do they create what is real?

Descartes tries to base religion on certain grounds and prove God's existence as a matter of speculative reason. God's existence as a nonphysical being can be proven with logic, according to Descartes. Knowledge in the physical sciences also employs observation, Descartes noted, but knowledge of God's existence can be known through logic alone. If Descartes were correct and God's existence were certain and rationally proven, a person who doubted the existence of God would not merely entertain a private belief. He or she would entertain an irrational belief, a wrongheaded view, and an insane position. Soren Kierkegaard, a critic of Descartes' approach, replies that people believe in God, not because the belief is rational, but because it is irrational.

The certainty that Descartes claimed for his proof of God's existence is closely linked to his dualist world view and his radical foundationalism. Speculative reason, according to Descartes, enabled him to establish the fact of God's existence.

Blaise Pascal

Blaise Pascal, a French philosopher, presents a pragmatic argument concerning religion. Pascal considers the various possibilities. Either God, as the term is understood in the Augustinian-Cartesian tradition, exists or God does not exist; either a person believes or does not believe.

He then considers the consequences of each of four possibilities. (1) If I believe and God exists, I will receive an eternal reward (heaven), but I will miss some good times on earth (by following God's commands). (2) If I don't believe and God exists, I will receive eternal punishment (hell), although I will have more good times on earth. (3) If I believe and God does not exist, there will be no eternal reward and I will have fewer good times on earth. (4) If I don't believe and God does not exist, I will receive no eternal punishment and will have more good times on earth.

Pascal then decides to avoid the worst possible outcome—eternal punishment. He can put up with missing some good times, but he is unwilling to take the risk of eternal punishment. The risks of unbelief, he decides, outweigh the benefits of unbelief; the benefits of belief outweigh the risks of belief. Pascal concludes that belief is the true course—since, according to the pragmatists, a belief is true if it has good results.

William James

In his essay "The Will to Believe," the American philosopher William James carves out a middle ground between what he calls religious absolutism and scientific absolutism. He rejects both forms of absolutism and the claims of certainty made by each. James finds that the religious certainty on the question of God's existence is associated with a correspondence (*adaequatio*) between the mind and reality.

Scientific absolutism takes the form of a strict application of the empiricist principle of verification. On this view, according to James, nothing is accepted as existing until it passes the test of public verification. According to the scientific absolutist, James reports, faith accepted in the absence of scientific verification is "the lowest form of immorality."

James accepts that uncertainty may accompany the religious claims that perfection is eternal and that it is better to believe than not to believe that perfection is eternal. Moral as well as religious belief, according to James, creates its own truth. In the moral arena, a person confident that he or she will receive a promotion makes a claim on the higher powers, as it were—a claim that can have the effect of bringing about the promotion. The confidence that one displays may actually be the factor that wins the appointment to the job. In religion, the belief that a personal world is a better world may bring about a more personal world.

James contends that the religious hypothesis should not be ruled out. While the certainty of those in religion who claim knowledge of the perfect and eternal realm is not warranted, beliefs that can bring about their own truth should not be ruled out.

Thomas Aquinas

Thomas Aquinas incorporates an Aristotelian approach as he turns to address the question of God's existence. He asks what, for practical purposes, may be known in regard to God's existence. He operates within the framework of practical reason. Unlike Descartes, he does not speculate on the ultimate nature or origin of things, but he accepts the prospect that human reason may be limited in its efforts to discover such ultimate truths.

Aquinas presents several arguments for the existence of God. I will consider the first-cause argument, based on Aquinas' "second way" or argument from efficient cause. The term "God" has multiple meanings: Aquinas draws upon a meaning distinctly different from Descartes' notion of a perfect being. Aquinas shares Aristotle's skepticism about the use of reason to know nonphysical forms. Like Aristotle, however, he accepts the use of reason that enables humans to engage in practices –that is, he accepts practical reason or practical wisdom as providing a basis for actions and policies. The Aristotelian tone of Aquinas' approach is evident in his use of the expression "efficient cause," one of Aristotle's four causes.

The first-cause argument is a version of the argument that Kant described as the cosmological proof for God's existence. As we grow and observe practices, we make some sense of our world by interpreting some events as causing other events. So we may think as follows. If something exists, it had a cause. The universe exists. So the universe had a cause (and whatever this cause is, that is what people refer to when they use the word 'God.')

The tone of this "proof" is quite different from the tone of certainty in Descartes. Aquinas in this argument is trying to make sense of a realm that lies beyond ordinary experience. We don't have direct experience of the origins of the universe, so we don't make claims to certainty concerning its origins. This realm may lie beyond the human ability to know with certainty.

According to the Canadian philosopher Etienne Gilson, Aquinas holds that to assign any human characteristics–such as father, creator, and judge–to an alleged cause of the universe is to anthropomorphize. Aquinas thus speaks of the eternal and the infinite. In using these terms, Aquinas does not refer to an indefinitely long span of time nor a set of objects too numerous to count. By "eternal" and "infinite" Aquinas refers rather to what is located neither in time nor space–what is non-temporal and non-finite.

Humans can know, for practical purposes, what is located in space and time. To claim knowledge of anything beyond space and time, however, is to claim knowledge of the unknown and perhaps unknowable. Knowledge of such a realm is speculative, not practical. The realm of the infinite and eternal, then, does not lie within the human capacity to know with certainty. The God of Aquinas, according to Gilson, is the unknown and perhaps unknowable God. Claims to know God's will with certainty are not fit to the dimensions of practical reason and may be unverifiable with speculative reason.

Critics of Aquinas' first-cause argument have offered their own speculations on this realm and replied that the argument does not prove only one cause of the universe. Something so complex may have had more than one cause. Perhaps the universe was made by committee.

William Paley

William Paley, an English theologian, gave a proof for God's existence known as the argument from design. This argument is also called the teleological argument. Aquinas gives a version of this argument in his "fifth way."

The argument may be stated as follows: Wherever there is design, there is a designer. There is design in the universe. Thus, the universe had a designer, and this designer people call God. In defense of the second premise ("there is design in the universe"), those who subscribe to this argument from design have cited the order, pattern, and regularity of the universe.

David Hume has challenged the argument from design. First, he maintains that order in the universe does not imply that the universe itself is orderly. What is true of a part, he maintains, is not necessarily true of the whole. Secondly, Hume contends that design does not necessarily imply a designer. Oak seeds regularly become oak trees and not evergreens, Hume observes. From this he concludes that order and regularity may be attributable to a sexual process. The universe may be a product of a sexual process, according to Hume, rather than the product of a designer or "great watchmaker."

David Walker

The voice of David Walker, an African-American who lived in Boston, identifies views of Anglo- and European-Americans that invite self-reflection. Walker, in his *Appeal in Four Articles; Together with a Preamble, to the Coloured Citizens of the World*, calls on slaves to overthrow the oppression of slavery. Challenging Jefferson's views on African-Americans, Walker compares the treatment of Africans in America to the treatment of slaves in ancient Egypt and Rome to demonstrate the unprecedented cruelty of the type of slavery practiced in the Americas. Slavery as practiced in the Americas was chattel slavery, which reduced humans to the level of "cattle" or property. In response to Jefferson's claims that Africans allegedly have lower physical and intellectual capacities than Europeans, Walker asks how well a caged deer could run in competition with another that had been able to run freely. Walker predicts that Jefferson's claim that the nature of Africans rather than their condition explains their inferior status will influence the views that many people adopt toward Africans. Walker argues that whites are avaricious people who are willing to treat others as mere property or to reduce others to the level of brutes for the purpose of gaining wealth and status. Walker appeals to blacks to seek self-government and to prove wrong the claims of men like Jefferson. Practices as cruel as slavery, Walker contends, will not go unpunished by God.

Walker's *Appeal* provides an illustration of religion exercised from the perspective of practical reason. The voice of the author in such writings is sometimes referred to as a prophetic voice, in which prophesy is viewed as "telling forth" the consciousness of the people. The people's consciousness in regard to slavery is that the profit motive or avarice has blinded the slave owners and those who invest in the slave trade to the inhumane consequences of reducing people to property. This view of prophesy may be contrasted with another view, in which prophesy is regarded as "foretelling" the future. Powers to foretell the future are associated in the minds of some people with higher powers allegedly known through speculative reason or special mental powers. While Walker's predictions did unfold in history, the insights they were based on reflected a practical understanding of the sense of fairness possessed by each person–slave as well as non-slave.

Part 4:

Feminist and Multicultural Perspectives

Chapter 9: Feminist Perspectives

In this chapter, feminist criticisms of specific philosophers are presented. Some authors who represent feminist perspectives–Simone de Beauvoir, Harriet Taylor, Annette Baier, Sara Ruddick, and Jean Grimshaw–have been included in previous chapters. The positions of Baier and Grimshaw are reviewed in this chapter.

On Plato

Lynda Lange

Lynda Lange considers the issue of whether Plato was a feminist. With this question she appears to ask whether Plato made equality of the sexes his main concern. She asserts that he was not a feminist since his main concern was the unity (or health) of the city-state.

In support of her claim that Plato was not a feminist, Lange points out that Plato's position that women could be trained for the role of guardian was prompted by his concern for the efficiency of the state. Efficiency was necessary for the state to attain unity or health.

Lange offers additional support for her thesis by drawing on a distinction between public and private spheres. She observes that Plato gave priority to the public and regarded the private sphere as less important. Plato, according to Lange, associated males with activities in the public and females with activities in the private sphere.

Lange also suggests an alternative to Plato's model of the state. She proposes that, instead of the view that the state is an individual organism, that the state be viewed as a family.

Susan Moller Okin

Susan Moller Okin gives a more sympathetic account of Plato's analysis than does Lange. Okin maintains that Plato incorporates an analysis of the family in his search for a model of political society. While Plato compares the political state to an individual person in his description of an ideal society, he sees the private family as the building block for the "second-best" society.

Okin attempts to locate Plato in his historical setting and finds that Plato's description of an ideal or best city in the *Republic* is a bold and radical attempt to challenge some of the established ways in Athens. She finds in Plato's *Laws* a description of a second-best city, which also challenges some of the established ways but in a less radical manner. The goal of political life, according to Plato, is to attain a just, harmonious state and to promote virtue and moral goodness in the citizens.

In Plato's ideal (best) city, the private family and private property are abolished among the class of leaders, the Guardians. Plato proposes that among the Guardians property, including wives and children, be held in common. The proposal that a commune of wives, children, and property be established among the Guardians abolishes the private family. The abolition of the private family requires that Plato re-define the role of women, according to Okin, and he suggests that women as well as men are capable of leadership in the public arena.

Plato's challenge to the existing structure of society in his ideal state traced the abilities of women to the training they had received for domestic functions. He proposed that if women were appropriately trained they would be as capable as males for leadership roles.

Okin warns against anachronism—reading the present into the past—in approaching the texts of Plato. Some of Plato's critics have objected strongly to the proposal that private families be eliminated. The deep emotional needs served by the family, according to this objection, would be unmet in the absence of a private family.

To raise this objection, Okin observes, is to be guilty of an anachronism. She points out that the family was not generally the source of the satisfaction of deep emotional needs in ancient Athenian society. It may have developed to serve these needs in more recent times, but in ancient Athens the family did not serve this function. One reason was that the woman did not choose her spouse but had her spouse chosen for her by father or brother. Plato, Okin notes, extends to males the inability to choose one's reproductive mate when he eliminates the family in the ideal society.

The second-best city in Plato's proposal does not abolish the private family. Plato concedes that in practice people are unable to give up the family, and in the *Laws* Plato outlines the structure and rules of a just society that includes the private family. In his description of the second-best city, however, Plato continues to challenge some of the existing practices in Athens. Women are given a more equal treatment in divorce laws, in laws regarding the wounding or murder of a spouse, and in laws regarding extramarital intercourse. Okin attributes Plato's promotion of more equal treatment for women in these legal matters to his view that a political society should make the citizens more virtuous and temperate.

Despite his rare attempt among philosophers to give a more equal status for women, Plato preserved the private family in his practical proposal in the *Laws*. In doing so, according to Okin, he retained one of the main impediments to full personhood for women in ancient Athens. The private family possessed heritable property, and the inheritance laws passed property through the male line. Women could not inherit real property, and the possession of property was a condition of being regarded as a person in Athenian society.

On Aristotle

Jean Bethke Elshtain

Jean Bethke Elshtain points to some weak points of the Aristotelian tradition in her account of the failure of the women's suffrage movement to achieve full equality for women. She maintains that suffragists bought into an Aristotelian model of power politics, but in doing so they unwittingly accepted a system that had become associated with class, race and sex oppression.

As suffragists described the problems they sought to correct and as they offered possible solutions, they associated the problems with public immorality and turned to private morality to find solutions. Since the public realm had traditionally been a male domain and the private realm a female domain, the suffragists associated men with immorality and women with morality. To address public problems, they sought to transfer moral values from the private into the public sphere.

The Aristotelian split between public and private realms located women in the private arena. Men, Aristotle held, were naturally suited to lead and women to follow. For this reason, men occupied both the public domain of politics as well as the private domain of family. Women, by contrast, were confined to the private realm of the family. In the well-governed city-state that Aristotle envisioned, a shared notion of the good life became the basis for public policy.

Over the centuries, the public-private division became more pronounced. Augustine, Machiavelli, and Jean Bodin linked the public or political realm with competition and immorality. A shared notion of the good life no longer provided the basis for public policy in the political arena. The suffragists failed to recognize this alteration of the Aristotelian model when they proposed that problems in the public arena could be resolved by transferring values from the private realm of the family to the public realm of politics.

Elshtain cautions that the acceptance of the public-private split places women in a double bind. Women enter the public arena with an Aristotelian notion that public life can be transformed if people adopt a shared notion of morality. However, the sharp public-private division of more recent centuries does not accept the Aristotelian notion that a shared notion of the good life is the basis of public policy. The result for women is that any talk about values–the health, education, and welfare of children, for example–reflects a concept of the good life in the private sphere, but by entering the public arena women have forfeited the right to defend these private values.

Elizabeth Spelman

Elizabeth Spelman describes Aristotle's position that men are superior to women and offers the criticism that Aristotle's argument is circular. Aristotle offered as his reason for the superiority of men over women that the rational element in humans was superior to the irrational element. He associated men with the rational element and women with the irrational.

Aristotle held that the human soul could not be known directly, so any claims about the soul had to be based on analogy. The analogy Aristotle used to depict the soul was that of relationships between people. To describe the relationship between males and females, he employed the political categories of superior and subordinate.

Spelman observes that Aristotle tried to ground his political position concerning the relationship between men and women on his metaphysical or psychological position regarding the human personality. The political position was that men are superior to women; the metaphysical or psychological position was that the rational in humans is superior to the irrational.

The circularity sets in when Aristotle argues for the view that the superiority of men over women rests on the superiority of the rational over the irrational. Aristotle bases his claim that men should control women on the underlying claim that the rational should control the irrational. He asserts that nature intended the rational to control the irrational, but he offers no support for this assertion. His claim that the soul can be known only by analogy leads Aristotle to use the language of political domination. To explain the superiority of the rational part of the soul over the irrational, Aristotle describes human beings who stand in relationships of power and authority. In doing so, he returns full circle to his starting point.

On Augustine

Rosemary Radford Ruether

Rosemary Radford Ruether finds both an attitude of misogyny and a promotion of virginity in Augustine's writings. The misogyny may be traced to Augustine's dualism. Things of the spirit were unified (monistic) and rational. The body in Augustine's view, however, represented a lower order of being. When the bodily appetites ruled the reason, disorder and chaos was the result–both in the individual organism and in society.

On the other hand, when reason directed the bodily appetites, the organism was healthy and society was well-ordered.

Augustine associated the bodily elements with the woman. In the order of nature, as conceived by Augustine, men should rule women. When men rule women, the higher order directs the lower order and harmony results.

Women were not, however, completely identified with the bodily appetites by Augustine. They also could overcome these appetites and be ruled by reason. The ideal state of life for a woman governed by her reason was the state of virginity. Convents were created for females and served the same purpose for women as monasteries served for men –to attain the ideal of monistic spirituality (from which "monastic" spirituality is derived) in which reason ruled over the body.

On Thomas Hobbes

Carole Pateman

Carole Pateman finds in Hobbes a patriarchal view that removes women from any political role. She acknowledges that Hobbes claims women are equal to men in the state of nature, but she detects behind Hobbes' claim an assumption that women have no significant place in political society.

Hobbes' argument reduces women to political non-entities. He initially describes women and men as equals in the state of nature, since any human who has a weapon can seriously harm and even kill another. Hobbes also assigns to a mother the right of dominion over her child in the state of nature; he gives as his reason that maternity is more easily and clearly established than paternity.

From this point on, however, the role of women is seriously curtailed by Hobbes. He defines a family in the state of nature as "a man and his children; or of a man and his servants; or of a man, and his children, and servants together; wherein the father or master is the sovereign." Hobbes, according to Pateman, reduces the male-female relationship to one of conquest. In the state of nature, the woman is part of a family, but her role is that of a servant to a male who has conquered her.

Pateman claims further that in Hobbes' state of civilization the woman disappears as a political entity. Because males play such a dominant role in the state of nature, only males negotiate the social contract. The result of the males-only negotiations is evident in the social contract. Conjugal rights are not rights possessed by females: they are possessed by males only. Conjugal rights in Hobbes' state of civilization are mainly reduced to rights of the male to subjugate the female.

On John Locke

Lorenne M. G. Clark

Lorenne Clark turns to John Locke to illustrate her thesis that western political philosophers assume male dominance over females. She maintains that this assumption eliminates the possibility of sexual equality from the theories of Western political philosophers. Locke's theory poses a special problem for her thesis, since Locke favors consent as the basis of human relationships.

Clark addresses the problem of Locke's favoring consent by saying that consent applies only to his state of civilization: in Locke's state of nature relationships are not voluntary. The laws of nature are not the products of consent, while the laws of civil society are the result of a social contract that is supported by mutual consent.

Locke, according to Clark, locates the reproductive relationship outside the social contract; in doing so, he accepts the domination of male by female rather than a consensual relationship in reproduction. He regards the family and the power relationships within it as natural. Locke also finds in nature a superiority of male over female based on the male's strength, a superiority that entitles husbands to the obedience of their wives.

As Clark interprets Locke, relationships of reproduction are governed by the laws of nature, not by the laws of civil society. She observes that Locke presumes superiority of some over others in relationships of production as well as relations of reproduction. In reproductive relationships, males have a "natural" superiority over females who depend on the males for survival. According to Clark, Locke maintains that "the ownership of the means and products of reproduction, as well as those of production, [is] what is really needed to generate the kind of political society which Locke thinks is needed to secure 'the peace, safety, and public good of the people,' which is, he argues, the end of government."

Clark regards Locke's main purpose in his theory to be the establishment of inheritance practices through the male line. She refers to Locke's objective of "legitimizing exclusive male control of inheritable property." She also writes: "His theory had two major objectives, the legitimizing of inequality in the distribution of property as between one man and another (or, more accurately, as between one family and another), and the legitimizing of an exclusive male right to control and dispose of familial property." Later she adds: "...a theory whose sole object is to ensure the individual right of men to appropriate, own, and control the future disposition of property...."

Clark finds certain points at which Locke seems to avoid the assumption that males naturally dominate females. Locke, for example, makes the marriage contract a matter of mutual consent. In addition, father and mother both share authority over the child. Clark explains away these apparent inconsistencies in Locke in the following way: "The joint authority of parents is...a theme he relentlessly repeats, and in fact, he goes as far as he can in denigrating the authority over children which paternity legitimizes, in order to undermine as far as possible patriarchal concepts of what constitutes legitimate government."

Clark goes on to maintain that in Locke the major function of marriage is to establish a mechanism for transferring property from one generation to the next. Locke, according to Clark, reduces the marital relationship to a property relationship. People come to own property by mixing their labor with resources. Those who are more industrious and exercise greater knowledge in this activity are entitled to more possessions. The male "owns" the female and the children in a family. Clark offers as evidence of this ownership the inheritance laws of England in the seventeenth century, in which property is inherited through the male line and females are not allowed to own property.

Locke regards women as mothers or wives and thereby leaves out single women in his discussion of property ownership. Women are viewed by Locke as less capable in the activity of mixing labor with resources; hence, they are less qualified to own property.

Mary Lyndon Shanley

Mary Lyndon Shanley provides a different interpretation of Locke than that given by Clark. Rather than view Locke as one who sought to justify the domination of men over women, Shanley places Locke in a historical setting and finds that he challenged a royalist interpretation of the social contract.

Locke, according to Shanley, represents a shift from a royalist to a liberal interpretation of the social contract. The marriage contract had been regarded by royalists as a model for the social contract between monarch and subjects. The royalists interpreted the husband-wife relationship as one of master to subject, in which the husband is superior and the wife is subordinate. The royalist interpretation of the choice to enter the marriage contract was that the parties choose whether to enter this relationship and to accept its traditional terms of superiority and subordination.

Locke gave a different interpretation of the marriage contract. Rather than view the contract as a permanent agreement to enter a traditional superior-subordinate relationship, Locke viewed it as a contract between people who are equal, or nearly equal, and who negotiate most of the terms of the contract.

Locke allowed for a temporary rather than a permanent contract. He regarded the main purpose of the marriage contract to be the raising of children. When that goal was attained, as Shanley interprets Locke, the marital relationship could be ended.

Locke's re-interpretation of the marriage contract supported his challenge to the royalist interpretation of the social contract. The social contract in Locke was drawn among equals who negotiated the terms of the contract. The social contract was not a permanent agreement between superior and subordinate but was re-negotiable.

On Immanuel Kant

Susan Mendus

Susan Mendus offers a criticism of Kant's view of women. She expresses a surprise shared by other contemporary philosophers as she approaches the writings of Kant. Kant is viewed by some as a major voice in modern liberal philosophy and a defender of individual rights; for this reason, it comes as a surprise to find in some of his writings a disparaging and condescending view toward women.

Kant regards male property owners and providers as active citizens, but he includes women among a class that he describes as "passive citizens." A passive citizen is one who does not look out for himself or herself, but is under the care and tutelage of another.

Kant does not view women as the equals of men in academic matters, nor does he find that women approach intimate relationships in the same way as do men. He regards women as more promiscuous than men.

Sexual relationships reduce humans to the level of animals, according to Kant, for the reason that such relationships reduce the sexual partner to an object. Since humans are entitled to be treated as subjects or ends-in-themselves, sexual intimacy denatures humans.

Mendus finds three possible explanations for these attitudes in Kant. First, she traces his views to attitudes prevalent in the Germany of his day.

Secondly, she finds a possible explanation for Kant's willingness to assign women a subordinate position in the need to keep the family together. Family relationships or relationships within organic communities can be harmonious only if one individual (or more) is subordinate to one as the head of the family. Since Kant is interested in preserving the family unit, he describes women as naturally subordinate to men.

Thirdly, Mendus traces Kant's description of male-female relationships to Kant's individualism. When humans are regarded as deserving of respect on the grounds that they are autonomous individuals, as Kant maintains, intimate and family relationships are reduced to domination and subordination.

Mendus concludes with a warning that individualism can lead to excesses and narrow-mindedness in our own time as well as it did in Kant's time. She finds that feminism can also fall into individualist excesses–by turning women into pseudo-men, for example. She advises that Kant's excesses serve as warnings for present-day individualists.

Annette Baier

Annette Baier's position on Kant is presented in Chapter Five above. Baier criticizes Kant and other liberals for making justice the first virtue of morality. Care for particular others, according to Baier, has a more central place in morality than it is assigned by liberal theorists. While Kant finds the choice of the rules by which humans govern themselves the motive of morality, Baier regards care in unchosen relationships as a central feature and a motive of morality.

On John Stuart Mill

Mary Lyndon Shanley

Mary Lyndon Shanley endorses Mill's position on equality for women in regard to suffrage, education, and employment, but she criticizes his failure to address equal division of domestic tasks and his view that most women would choose marriage. She finds the main strengths of his position to be the promotion of friendship in marriage and his criticism of the corruption of the male-female relationship.

Shanley interprets Mill as promoting community in his description of marriage and as defending non-instrumental relationships within marriage. Rather than turning to equal opportunity for women, Mill is said to have based equality in marriage on equality between males and females. Such equality is necessary if friendship is to be present in marriage and if progress is to be made in human society.

On Karl Marx

Heidi Hartmann

Heidi Hartmann finds some shortcomings in the Marxist alliance with feminism. She sees in the alliance that feminism is reduced to the struggle against capitalist exploitation. While men have fought against exploitation by capital, Hartmann proposes, women must fight against both capitalist exploitation and patriarchy. Women can add to the struggle the importance of interdependence and nurture, values that rationalist and competitive men are unable to bring to the struggle for liberation.

Hartmann accepts the material explanation of things that Marx advances. Relationships within society and between the sexes are understood by Marx as having solely material causes. The capitalist system as well as the patriarchal system, for example, can be fully explained in terms of the economic forces of production and the behavioral factors of domination.

As a Marxist, Hartmann shares the belief that conflict is the natural state between the classes and between the sexes; however, civilization can produce peace between both warring classes and battling sexes. Society can do so by establishing procedures that assure equal distribution of the wealth and equal treatment of women.

The task is complicated by the dual goal of feminists, who may not be liberated in the same way that workers are liberated. Hartmann explains that an alliance between capitalists and patriarchal union leaders supported "family wages" during the early years of industrialization. This legislation was aimed at protecting families: it countered the practice of capitalists to employ women and children, as well as men, in an effort deliberately to keep wages low. The concept of the family wage allowed wages for men that were high enough to support a family, but it also allowed lower wages for women. The effect, according to Hartmann, was that women were denied a realistic choice to enter the work force. The raising of children in marriage was their only alternative if women were to survive.

Men are liberated when they are freed from capitalist exploitation, according to Hartmann, but women must be liberated from both capitalist exploitation and the patriarchy of family wages.

Jane Humphries

Jane Humphries challenges several features of Marx's argument concerning the family. She also gives a different interpretation of the family wage law from that offered by Heidi Hartmann. Marx gave a materialist explanation of the family and linked it closely with capitalism. The paternalism of capitalism, according to Marx, was a reflection of male domination in the family. Marx predicted that the paternalistic family would decline along with capitalism.

Humphries finds that during two centuries of capitalism in Great Britain the family has not suffered the fate that Marx predicted and she tries to explain why this is so. Humphries adopts a materialist perspective, but she provides a less individualistic account of human needs than that given by Marx. The family structure, in Humphries' view, allowed working families to preserve a standard of living, to control the number of workers, and to achieve cohesion in carrying on the class struggle.

According to Humphries, Marx's challenge to the private family and his expectation that communism would bring an end to the paternalistic family failed to take into account the foundational nature of the family in society. Care for the young, the elderly, and the disabled was provided by the family in pre-capitalist societies, in which every member of the family made a contribution in some form. Both traditionally and among 19th-century radicals, care for nonlaboring members of the family was viewed as part of the social contract between the classes. Outside assistance for children and the elderly was expected by working families as a matter of right.

During the early phases of industrial capitalism, families came under threat from the deliberate policies of wage and welfare controls by the governing class. The New Poor Law of 1834 kept the living conditions of those in the poor house more squalid than the living conditions of those working for the lowest wages. Managers deliberately hired women and children at wages lower than the wages of male heads of families to drive wages down—including the wages of male heads of households.

Under these conditions of poor house squalor and exploitative wages, the family wage was sought as a way to preserve the family and its quality of life. This was a wage that provided enough for the head of the household to support the nonlaboring members of the family. An adequate family wage could be shared with the young, the elderly, and the needy in the family. Education could be given to the young when they were not forced by need into the workplace. Necessary domestic work could be done by mothers if they were not compelled to earn wages in the factory or mine. The family wage was thus sought to preserve the family's quality of life. It was not aimed at preserving a system of male dominance in the working class.

In addition to preserving the quality of life, Humphries argues, the cohesiveness of the working family also allowed the working class to control the number of laborers available to the workforce. In Marx's explanation, the working class family functioned to provide workers for the workforce. Humphries, however, describes a more significant role for the family. Labor's struggle for the family wage gave some control of the number of workers available. The intent of the family wage was to provide sufficient wages to the head of the household so that the young, the elderly, and those such as the mother who were needed to perform domestic functions could remain in the home. By remaining at home, mothers and children were not available to be hired in the workplace. A second effect of the family wage movement, then, was to control the number of laborers in the workplace.

The final role of the working family that Humphries describes is that it was not simply a perpetrator of capitalist manners and values. The commitment to family often stimulated members of the working class to engage in class struggle against the governing class. Bread riots led by women to keep down the cost of bread provide an example of such action.

On John Rawls

Susan Moller Okin

Susan Moller Okin examines the theory of John Rawls and finds some difficulties for the equal treatment of women; however, she proposes that his powerful account can be modified and employed to serve the cause of equality for women.

Okin contends that Rawls leaves out half of the world's population in his account of justice. Rawls regards the negotiators of the social contract as heads of families. In doing so, however, he leaves out other adults who are members, but not heads, of families. In most cases these others turn out to be women.

Part of her evidence that Rawls leaves out women as subjects of justice is that people learn their place as wage-earners when the veil of ignorance is lifted or, in the language of the Rawls Game, when the cards are turned upright. Many or most women, when the veil is removed, discover their place to be that of a non-wager-earner. The slavery that had been ruled out from behind the veil of ignorance is imposed on a large class of women.

Rawls also leaves out the family as an institution that should be governed by the principles of justice. Although he indicates in his initial sketch of his theory that the family is a basic institution of society, he fails to provide any detail on how justice should be applied within the family.

Rawls distinguishes religious and other voluntary associations from the institution of the family. While people voluntarily enter into churches and similar communities, one does not choose to be born into a family. Okin offers this as a reason that Rawls should include the family as an institution to be governed by the principles of justice. The effects of the natural lottery in family membership, according to Okin, may be softened if rules of justice are applied to families.

Jean Grimshaw

Jean Grimshaw, in Chapter Five above, identifies Rawls' theory as a male approach to morality often associated with the public arena. She contrasts this with an approach represented by Carol Gilligan and Nel

Noddings–an ethics of care that emphasizes the preservation of relationships–that is more closely linked to a female or private morality. Grimshaw expresses confidence that these alternative approaches to morality may be complementary as women and men work together in the public arena.

On Alasdair MacIntyre

Elizabeth Frazer and Nicola Lacey

Elizabeth Frazer and Nicola Lacey agree that Alasdair MacIntyre's communitarian position is an improvement on the individualism and empiricism that underlie mainstream liberalism, but they challenge some features of MacIntyre's account of practices. Their specific challenge is that MacIntyre fails to provide an adequate account of change and development within practices. Feminist successes in changing the role of women in heterosexual relationships, for example, illustrate that the process of change within practices is more complex than MacIntyre allows. Further, MacIntyre is unable to account for evil practices.

MacIntyre, according to Frazer and Lacey, holds that practices develop in a fairly peaceful way. They change in response to criticism, in MacIntyre's view, that aims more fully to define and clarify the practice. Frazer and Lacey point out that change within practices and traditions sometimes involves greater upheaval than MacIntyre describes. At issue in feminist advances, for example, has been the question of who has input to change a tradition or a practice. The question of what constitutes goods internal to a practice, in the argument advanced by Frazer and Lacey, depends on particular perspectives. The good of male dominance in the traditional family, in heterosexual relationships, in university appointments, and so forth depends on whether one adopts a male or a female perspective. The definition of internal goods, then, results from a more complex process than MacIntyre allows.

MacIntyre finds that virtues arise from the pursuit of goods internal to practices. Some activities may qualify as practices but may also be evil. Frazer and Lacey point to MacIntyre's failure to take into account the complexity of practices as partly responsible for his inability to identify and reject evil practices.

Marilyn Friedman

Marilyn Friedman criticizes the communitarian claim of Alasdair MacIntyre and others that personal identity is derived from a community that one has not chosen. She argues in favor of going beyond the identities formed by family, neighborhood, church, and national communities. While one may be influenced by these communities, a person's identity need not be totally shaped by them. An individual can go beyond these communities to chosen or "dislocated" communities.

Friedman describes urban communities as modern voluntary communities. Small minorities, ethnic groups, and subcultures constitute some of these urban communities. One's identity may be formed by these voluntary associations to a greater extent than the unchosen community (or communities) in which one was born and raised. "The modern self may seek new communities whose norms and relationships stimulate and develop her identity and self-understanding more adequately than her unchosen community of origin, her original community of place."

Chapter 10: Multicultural Perspectives

So far in this book, we have examined Anglo-American and European (AAE), Afro-American, and feminist philosophies. When AAE cultures have faced such issues as overpopulation and social conflict, the typical solution has been to move out to a frontier and to establish colonies. "Go west, young man," was Horace Greeley's mandate that encapsulated this approach toward managing the problems. While exceptions are found, it may be said that over the millenia many other cultures have "stayed at home" and addressed social ills. Asian, African, Arabic, Native American and various other indigenous populations, which I will refer to as "non-AAE" cultures, have tended to address social problems without turning to expansionism.

One result of the different practices of emigration is that AAE cultures have made major contributions to science and technology, while non-AAE cultures have made their main contributions to social and political philosophy. When AAE peoples encountered the harsh life of the frontier, having firepower and other means of conquering natural and human obstacles was useful. "Necessity was the mother of invention" in the new world frontiers.

In the non-AAE cultures, by contrast, tools of excessive domination probably posed more of a threat than a benefit. When people are trying to continue to live together, perhaps in crowded circumstances, introducing guns and bullets can be a hindrance. The discovery of gunpowder in China, for example, led to the creation of fireworks, not bullets. Social and political philosophies in the non-AAE cultures have tended to provide more detailed proposals for attaining social harmony than have the AAE philosophies.

As the frontiers for new settlements disappear on the planet, the social and political philosophies of non-AAE traditions may significantly contribute to understanding ways to deal with social ills– ways that have previously not occurred to or have not been available to people in the AAE traditions. Common to the non-AAE traditions are ancient religions that have remained to the present day and continue to exercise influence on populations. In the non-AAE traditions, the meaning of the term "religion" will be quite broad and different in many respects from the notion of religion in the AAE traditions. A practical orientation, to give one example, is detectable in each of the ancient traditions outlined in this chapter.

Some of the main difficulties with religious, communitarian AAE traditions have been the tyranny of orthodoxy and the tyranny of perfectionism. We have also seen that moral liberalism in the AAE traditions can suffer from a tyranny of the majority and a tyranny of the minority. The non-AAE traditions will now be examined for the help that they offer AAE traditions in addressing these difficulties. The benefits of this study may be mutual when common elements are found in the different cultures.

We will examine traditions in which the perspective of fairness seems to be a common element. Many traditions have viewed the fair-minded approach as a way to preserve peace. We will focus on each tradition's answer to the questions "Why should the perspective of fairness be adopted?" and "Who is capable of fair-mindedness?"

Confucianist Perspectives

Mandate of Heaven

In the Confucian tradition, the concept known as the Mandate of Heaven addresses the issue of good government. Confucianists claim that if the leaders fail to follow virtue the society will deteriorate or collapse. The Mandate of Heaven may be taken to mean that if the leaders fail to adopt the fair-minded perspective, the people themselves will do so. However, when the people are forced by intolerable circumstances to take fairness matters into their own hands, much suffering can result. The Mandate of Heaven contains a strong warning that when the people become sufficiently frustrated with the leaders civil war can result.

Confucianists trace the causes of civil wars to the failure of leaders to follow the virtuous ways of the ancients. The good leader, in Mencius' account, does not accept the suffering of the people. The good leader performs the rituals. The good leader is viewed as one who anticipates conflict and tries to head it off before the conflict has a chance to take shape. The good leader does not use the strong arm. If civil strife breaks out, the strife itself is an indication of a failure of leadership.

The Mandate of Heaven is the command that arises from the people's will. If the students and the workers oppose a policy, the leaders must take heed. The students may face a long lifetime under the policies established by the rulers, and the workers are often the first to suffer from specific policies. So the leaders must pay particular attention to the responses of these two groups as "first warnings" of the people's will.

Confucianism has sometimes been described as a moral philosophy rather than a religion. This classification may be accounted for in the following way. Some AAE religions claim that fairness is the way to attain the good life, but Confucianism adopts the fairness perspective mainly to avoid harm. "Do not do unto others what you would not have them do unto you" is the Confucian version of the Golden Rule. The avoidance of harm rather than the doing of good places limits on people's actions in this version.

While the Confucian version of the Golden Rule seems to allow much latitude for individual conceptions of the good life, Confucianists view the individual as inseparable from a community. As a member of a social organism, the individual shares a notion of the good life with others in the community, and a shared conception of the good life allows social stability.

Mencius regards people as basically good and the people's judgment as the most likely source of policies that will result in peace. Hsun-tzu, by contrast, views people as basically bad, but their evil tendencies can be corrected by education and training in virtue.

We have seen the debate in the AAE tradition between the Platonists and the Aristotelians. The Platonists generally hold that most people are short-sighted, self-interested and corrupt, and must be led by the few who can be fair-minded and protect the welfare of all. The Aristotelians, on the other hand, view people as basically good and allow that good government can be achieved in a polity–that is, a state in which the many govern. Moral liberalism and political individualism in the AAE traditions have had their roots in the Aristotelian optimism that the people in some cases are capable of governing themselves.

The debate within the Confucian tradition has some parallels with the debate between the Platonists and Aristotelians in the West. If the people are basically good, the views of the students and the workers can be trusted. Further, the leaders must heed these views if peace in society is to be sustained. However, if the people are basically bad, only the select few can govern and the many must be led away from their evil or self-interested ways. In this respect, the positions of

Confucius and Mencius are closer to the Aristotelian conception of the state while that of Hsun-tzu is closer to the aristocratic conception of the state found in Plato.

Filial Piety

Confucianists view the community as a social organism rather than as a social pyramid or an individual organism. The self-renewing community has a life just as a thriving family has a life. In the Confucian tradition, the family has a central economic, political and social role. When leaders govern the country as parents direct the family, the society is orderly. Disorder in the state results in disorder among families; when families are in good order, the state has internal harmony.

In *The Classic of Filial Piety*, Confucius is asked whether a filial child is always (simply) obedient to the parent. Confucius replies that if a king or a minister is to remain in office, he must be surrounded by those who would remonstrate–or debate the wisdom of policies–with him. Likewise, when a parent engages in unrighteous conduct, a child who fails to question the parent does not exercise filial piety.

A rival of Confucius, Mo Tzu, advocates an ethic of universal love in which one regards others as oneself. He then responds to several criticisms of his universal love position.

Some critics argue that the interests of one's own city should be placed before those of other cities. Mo Tzu replies that partiality toward one's own city is the source of many calamities; in answer to the critics, he contends that one who adheres to universal love would regard the interests of other states as equal to the interests of one's own.

A related criticism of Mo Tzu is that one must look out for one's own family first. Mo Tzu responds by describing two individuals, one who places the interests of his own family first and one who places the interests of everyone above those of his own family. He contends that the head of a family who faces his own death would prefer that his family be raised by the individual who favors the interests of everyone.

Other critics would hold that the better ruler is one who looks after himself. Mo Tzu replies that between two rulers–one who looks after the food and shelter of his people and another who does not–people would favor the one who looks after the people's needs.

Mo Tzu responds to still another group of critics who maintain that filial piety requires that children should first take care of their own parents. He replies that, in a social climate where love replaces hatred toward others, one's parents will be better cared for should a child be unable to care for his or her own parents.

Following the Confucian tradition, the Japanese author Nakae Toju writes that filial piety distinguishes the human from the nonhuman animal. In the Platonic tradition, by contrast, family love is regarded as the type of love that brings humans closest to the animals.

The Japanese have drawn upon the Confucian family model and made allegiance to the Emperor a matter of filial piety. In the Ministry of Education's 1937 publication *Fundamentals of Our National Polity*, filial piety is extended to the nation itself. The Imperial Household is regarded as the head family and the nucleus of national life.

In the AAE traditions, the spectrum of moral positions runs from the individual to the community: either the isolated individual is the moral agent or the community is the moral agent. AAE communitarians are divided over whether the universal human community or a smaller community (church or state) is the primary moral agent. In Confucian thought, the notion of an isolated individual is almost incoherent. The individual has no moral or political identity separate from the family or clan. In the East, the main division is over whether the family or the state is the primary moral agent.

In the twentieth century, Mao Tse-tung attempted to remove the family's central role in the economic and political life of China and to assign a primary role to the communist state. He accomplished this by appealing to class loyalties and class ideology. His reforms, however, apparently have been short-lived. A Confucianist revival that has attempted to restore the family as the basic economic unit has occurred since Mao's death.

Buddhist Perspectives

Buddhism proposes four Noble Truths as its starting point. The first is that suffering or sorrow exists. The second is that suffering has identifiable causes. The third noble truth is that suffering can be ended. The fourth is that the way to end suffering is through enlightened living –that is, by following the Eightfold Path. The steps on the Eightfold Path are right view, right aim, right speech, right action, right living, right effort, right mindfulness, and right contemplation.

Siddharta Gotama

Siddharta Gotama, the Buddha, was not an author. Although he wrote nothing, his followers wrote extensively about the Buddha and his teachings. Among the texts written by the followers is *The Dhammapada* (*Way of Virtue*).

According to the Buddha, the way to end suffering is through enlightenment and nirvana. The Eightfold Path can free one from clinging to pleasures, to doctrines, and to existence itself. At the center is emptiness. Once emptiness is realized, one cannot describe it. If one describes it, one has not realized it.

The way to enlightenment seems to be strictly private and to reduce one to silence. Apparently the individual alone frees himself or herself from cravings. In the main Buddhist traditions, however, the awareness of suffering becomes the basis of the treatment of others. The presence of suffering is offered as a reason for following the Golden Rule:

All are frightened of the rod.
Of death all are afraid.
Having made oneself the example,
One should neither slay nor cause to slay.

All are frightened of the rod.
For all, life is dear.
Having made oneself the example,
One should neither slay nor cause to slay.
(*The Dhammapada*, 129-130)

Why be fair-minded? The Buddhist answers "because people suffer." While enlightenment in Hinduism is directly available only to members of the Brahmin or priestly class, enlightenment in Buddhism is available to anyone.

Who is capable of fair-mindedness? Each person is capable of suffering; the experience of suffering, in turn, enables one to turn be fair-minded when deciding which actions to take toward others. If a person imagines himself or herself in the role of the victim ("having made oneself the example"), he or she is then in a position to act fairly toward others. So everyone should be fair-minded.

The tyranny of orthodoxy can take the form of divisions over who is capable of fair-mindedness. Buddhists seek to avoid this form of tyranny–or arbitrary treatment of some people by other people–by holding that everyone is capable of adopting the timeless perspective. Each person who suffers can be fair-minded. Suffering is the first of the basic truths of life. It is a starting point of conscious existence, an experiential truth. One need only turn to one's experience to find a starting point for morality and justice. This starting point can, in turn, prevent debates over who is capable of fairness–since anyone who suffers is capable of doing so. Because the issue of who can be fair-minded is settled in favor of the many and not merely the few in Buddhism, one of the main conflicts that leads to the tyranny of orthodoxy is avoided.

E. F. Schumacher

E. F. Schumacher in *Small Is Beautiful: Economics as if People Mattered* turns to Buddhist economics for a middle way between "materialist heedlessness" and "traditionalist immobility." He traces the causes of several current problems to the materialism of western economics–the collapse of the rural economy, a rising tide of unemployment in town and country, and the growth of a city proletariat without nourishment for either body or soul. Schumacher sees the dependency on distant fuel and food sources as an occasion of violence: people dependent on distant resources are more likely to engage in politically motivated violence than people who rely on local resources. When fuel sources are non-renewable–as they are with coal, oil and natural gas–the anxiety over their disappearance adds to the atmosphere of violence.

Schumacher contrasts the materialist economics of much Western thought with Buddhist economics. Western materialist economics measures success by the quantity of consumption: the more the better. Buddhist economics measures success by the ratio of result to resource. The practice that produces the greatest amount of benefit from the smallest amount of resources is the successful practice.

Materialist economics seeks to satisfy people's preferences; Buddhist economics attempts to fulfill people's nature. As a result, no limit is placed on the use and abuse of resources to satisfy people's desires in materialist economics. Conservation of resources, however, is at the heart of the Buddhist relationship to the environment.

Schumacher observes that work is regarded as an evil in western economics and thus is to be minimized. In Buddhist economics, however, work is balanced with leisure. In proper balance, work and leisure enable humans to realize their potentials.

Local economies, according to Schumacher, are more conducive to peace and non-violence than global economies. The middle way sought by Buddhists raises an issue of right livelihood–one of the steps on the Eightfold Path. Right livelihood includes an economy that is self-renewing. Only with a self-renewing economy, Schumacher contends, can stability in society be attained and placed in balance with personal freedom.

Hindu Perspectives

Hinduism was the mother culture from which Buddhism arose. In contrast to the Buddhist claim that nirvana or enlightenment is available to everyone, Hindus generally hold that only members of the priestly or Brahmin class are eligible for nirvana. A person lower on the social scale–in the warrior and worker-farmer castes and the "untouchables" or outcasts–must be reincarnated as a Brahmin before they may attain enlightenment.

Sarvepelli Radhakrishnan

The Hindu tradition has incorporated a caste system based on the notion of a scale or order of being. Sarvepelli Radhakrishnan describes the good, meaningful, and purposeful life as a life viewed as an organic whole. The past is linked to the future in a good life. He compares life to a game of cards–specifically, the game of bridge. We do not choose our own hand, but play with the cards we are dealt (the past). A player faces choices (the future) when a hand is dealt, and the number of choices is reduced as the game progresses. A good player, however, can discover more alternatives than a poor player–even in the later stages of the game. If the game is lost with poor play, the player cannot blame solely the hand that was dealt. The player's choices also contributed to the loss.

At first glance, a caste system seems to have unfairness built into it. Radhakrishnan's explanation, however, allows for a certain fairness in the outcome of the card game. A player's success depends in part on the decisions made in the course of the game. Radhakrishnan's proposal rests on a perfectionist notion of justice, in which some people are viewed as having greater potential than others. In Radhakrishna's perfectionism, not only are some people dealt better hands than others; some people also develop their skills more fully than others. The outcome in the distribution of social goods is not equal, but the outcome may be altered to a degree by an individual's choices. The outcome thus reflects both the organic nature of life and the individual's choices. In this respect, according to Radhakrishna, the outcome is fair.

Can fairness be attained in Hinduism? Rawls in the AAE tradition claims to reject a perfectionist notion of justice: the purpose of adopting the fair-minded perspective in the Rawlsian model is to mitigate the effects of the natural lottery. Radhakrishnan leaves the effects of the natural lottery in place: the individual must rely on his or her wit to play out the life game. Consolation for the disadvantaged is found in the doctrine of reincarnation. By living a moral existence, people may come back in a higher class. Living immorally, they may be condemned to come back in a lower class or even as an animal. The fair-minded perspective is available only to the few for policy decisions in Hinduism. The Brahmin or priests are educated in higher matters and can attain enlightenment: for this reason, only they are viewed as capable of seeing in a fair-minded way what is best for society.

The tyranny of orthodoxy is a grave danger when only the few are viewed as capable of adopting the timeless perspective. Included in the higher knowledge of the Brahmin is the realization that the natural lottery is directed by Brahman, the ruler of the universe. Some people are given natures that enable them to rule, others are best suited by nature for service. Virtue is accepting one's fate in the natural lottery and leading an existence that can bring one back higher in the order of being. When the state of enlightenment is achieved, the cycle of death and reincarnation is ended.

One might question whether the perspective of fairness is adopted–even by the few–for policy decisions in a caste system. It seems that the picture of truth and reality is quite straightforward: the law of survival of the fittest operates and the fittest class survives. This view, however, would seem to result in continual warfare. If self-interest were the motivator, the resentment that would result from extreme class divisions would prompt a war. In Thomas Hobbes' terms, this would be a war of everyone against everyone. Indian society has not experienced the perpetual struggle that one would expect if a Hobbesian perspective were adopted. To explain the ability of Indian society to renew itself for so many centuries, a fair-minded perspective that accepts an inequality in the distribution of goods and power in society is needed. In other words, an unequal distribution is viewed as fair. The Hindus have accepted that the natural lottery of talents sometimes does not match the distribution of social goods. This apparent injustice can be accepted if the belief is shared that injustices will be rectified in time through a process of rebirth and eventual attainment of nirvana through moral living. A shared belief in reincarnation helps to explain the stability of Hindu culture.

The tyranny of orthodoxy is avoided in Hinduism by an acceptance of a shared belief. The widely shared belief in reincarnation and eventual nirvana allows people to accept their place in the social hierarchy. One's fate is not under his or her control during the present life; good character may improve one's fate in the next reincarnation.

Mohandas Gandhi

Mohandas Gandhi was a major figure in the withdrawal of British rule from India during the middle years of the twentieth century. He studied in England and came to know the ideals of the English well. His understanding of both the Indian and British traditions helps to explain the appeal of Gandhi's philosophy.

Gandhi did not settle for speculative thought. "Thoughts without potency are airy nothings and end in smoke," he wrote. He regarded practical truth or reason–"living thought which awaits translation into speech and action"–as the avenue to enduring change.

He regarded the principle of satyagraha as the standard of right action. Gandhi claimed that satyagraha, the principle of non-violence, contained the power of the truth to overcome evil and oppression. He rejected the principles of might makes right and survival of the fittest since they were contradictory to the principle of satyagraha. "Non-violence is an active principle of the highest order," he wrote. "It is soul-force (*brahmana dharma*) or the power of the godhead within us.... Non-violence or soul-force...does not need physical aids for its propagation or effect. It acts independently of them. It transcends time and space."

The primary moral agent, according to Gandhi, is the *satyagrahi* who expresses compassion for his or her antagonist. The *satyagrahi* as a member of the human community is the moral agent. "The basic principle on which the practice of non-violence rests is that what holds good in respect of yourself holds good equally in respect of the whole universe. All mankind in essence are alike.... We are born as human beings in order that we may realize God who dwells within our hearts. This is the basic distinction between us and the beasts."

The function of a just state or just policy, in Gandhi's account, is to allow individual development–as a family supports the development of its members. "What is true of family must be true of society which is but a larger family."

The motive of morality, in Gandhi's account, is to release the power of the truth of nonviolence, of the soul-force, and thereby to prevent the destruction of the world. People should pursue non-violence to "conquer our conquerors." People are by nature non-violent, he wrote. To engage in non-violence is to engage in God-realization. "God-realization means seeing Him in all beings. Or, in other words, we should learn to become one with every creature."

Satyagraha, according to Gandhi, is the means to freedom. "The attainment of freedom," he wrote, "whether for a man, a nation or the world, must be in exact proportion to the attainment of non-violence by each." The few who perceive that *satyagraha* is the appropriate means to freedom have a duty to the many. "Let those...who believe in non-violence as the only method of achieving real freedom," Gandhi wrote, "keep the lamp of non-violence burning bright in the midst of the present impenetrable gloom. The truth of a few will count, the untruth of millions will vanish even like chaff before a whiff of wind."

The good life, in Gandhi's view, was the life of non-violence. "If we take recourse to *satyagraha*, we can conquer our conquerors the English, make them bow before our tremendous soul-force, and the issue will be of benefit to the whole world."

Gandhi assigned a primary place to virtue, and the overriding virtues were non-violence and love. The *yogi* or virtuous person is "'placid equally in affluence and adversity'" and "has 'neither attachment, nor greed nor the intoxication of status'.... In the ultimate resort it is the power of love that acts even in the midst of the clash and sustains the world."

African Perspectives

When various African and European cultures came into contact, some of the views of Christianity were met with perplexity. Chinua Achebe observes that the Igbo regarded the Christian notion of a loving God as too narrow. The Igbo held that God is a loving God when one is in God's favor; however, when one is out of God's favor, God is an angry god.

Among the Igbo and other African cultures, philosophy is passed from one generation to the next with the use of proverbs. Chinwe Okechukwu draws upon this tradition in her novel *The Predicament*. From the Igbo (or Ibo) culture she incorporates the proverb "A hen that has got its young ones with her does not fly to the top of a tree to sleep." A person is more cautious, according to this proverb, once she or he has responsibilities. This reflects the practice in the Igbo culture that the major civic responsibilities are given to married persons.

Another example: "The chicken that is walking along the roadside does not know that leaves have ears." One who speaks carelessly and in an unguarded fashion, this proverb teaches, may unwittingly fuel rumors.

Desmond Tutu and Frantz Fanon represent alternative responses to Anglo-European colonialism. Tutu defends nonviolence as a means to end colonialism, while Fanon regards violent opposition as the appropriate response to the injustices of colonial exploitation.

Desmond Tutu

In Desmond Tutu's account, everyone is capable of adopting a timeless, impartial perspective. A shared belief that colonial oppression and apartheid are wrong can unite the perpetrators as well as the victims of the policy of apartheid. A fair-minded perspective is regarded as a condition of freedom from oppression. If fair-mindedness can be achieved, violence can be avoided. A shared belief or shared conception of the good life must be present before a fair, impartial view can be adopted. The view that some people are denied their essential humanity or another equally forceful conviction must be shared before the fair-minded perspective can be adopted. The motive for adopting the fairness perspective was expressed by Tutu on the ABC television show *Nightline*. He commented in regard to the aftermath of apartheid in South Africa: "Without forgiveness, there is no future."

In a talk at a 1990 South African conference of churches, Tutu explained that forgiveness for apartheid was necessary to preserve humanness. Some of the difficulties of seeking forgiveness in a national setting became apparent during the conference. When he accepted the apology of a representative of the Dutch Reform Church, Tutu was accused by some of his followers of speaking for himself and not for others. In his reply to the charge, Tutu cited the suffering voices that he had heard and his effort to represent them. Tutu's sustained efforts were a major factor in the transition from a South African government that accepted apartheid to a government committed to an end of apartheid.

Tutu was aware that care must be exercised in adopting the fairness perspective for the reason that some people may not share the view that an injustice is present. Some may regard class and racial divisions as a natural state of affairs. Tutu realized that in the European tradition leadership was thought to be in the blood. If leadership were indeed hereditary, revolutions to overturn aristocratic leadership would run contrary to the natural or even the divine order of things. Tutu challenged this view by appealing to the egalitarian and non-violent elements in Christianity.

Frantz Fanon

According to Frantz Fanon, the colonial world of settler and native must be turned upside down. When it is inverted, as he indicates, "the first shall be last and the last first." Fanon seems to regard any shared perspective of fairness as impossible. He asserts that those who make such proposals are moral teachers who act as "bewilderers" of the native, exploited people. Direct action in the form of violent opposition is needed to invert the upright social pyramid. No timeless, impartial perspective is involved, according to Fanon; people mature into human adults politically and morally when they throw off the shackles that keep them in bondage and prevent their freedom.

Islamic Perspectives

Who can be fair-minded? In Islam, everyone who accepts the faith is capable of fair-mindedness. Islam does not accept class division. For this reason, a class of individuals who earn their living performing priestly duties is not permitted. The priestly class has been eliminated from Islam; in its place is found a universal priesthood of all believers. Each Muslim is a caliph or priest in the Islamic tradition.

If only some are regarded as capable of fair-mindedness, a priestly class can develop—as it has in various European societies. The few in this class can lord it over the others, and class division with priests in the highest class can develop. The impartial perspective can be adopted in Islam by all believers. When all are capable of adopting the timeless, impartial perspective, class division can be avoided.

Why should the perspective of fairness be adopted? The avoidance of class division prompts the adoption of the impartial, fair-minded perspective. Everyone is equal in the eyes of God (Allah). According to Allah's way, practices that result in human inequality are wrong. Since the charging of interest is a practice that can lead to some people becoming wealthy at the expense of others, according to some Muslim sects, the practice of charging interest is contrary to Allah's will.

Abu'l A'la Mawdudi

Abu'l A'la Mawdudi contends that the fair-minded perspective is adopted to avoid the social disorder of capitalist, communist, and fascist societies. Capitalist democracies separate religious considerations from public policy. As a result, policies that permit vice are capriciously voted in or out by the citizens. Vices proscribed by divine command–gambling, financial speculation, and the consumption of alcohol–are not permitted in Islam. Communism fails to protect the minorities within its borders since the needs of the majority prevail. Islam, Mawdudi contends, protects all its citizens since all are children of Allah. The Islamic state thus steers a middle course between capitalist democracy and communism.

The fascist state deteriorates into a dictatorship. While the Islamic state may resemble a dictatorship, its leader, the Amir, is not a dictator. The believers transfer their caliphate to the Amir for administrative purposes: if the leader fails to stay within the bounds of Allah's law or comes to regard himself as the source of authority, the leadership is tyrannical.

Why should care be taken in adopting a fair-minded perspective? If people who do not accept the Islamic faith are permitted a voice in fundamental policy, Mawdudi holds, social disorder can result. Believers can follow the divine way of moderation, but unbelievers are prone to follow self-interest and caprice. For this reason, only persons who accept the faith can exercise a vote. Non-Muslims are not to be regarded as inferior or unequal; they are not, however, permitted to exercise any say in basic policy matters.

Abdullah Ahmed An-Na'im

Abdullah Ahmed An-Na'im contends that national sovereignty makes the protection of human rights a rather complicated matter. Sovereign states must uphold human rights, but they can also impede the protection of human rights. This complex role of the sovereign state keeps the theory of human rights at odds with the practice of human rights.

Some nations that were under colonial rule when the human rights conventions were formulated in the 1940s were not represented in the original formulation of the rights. These countries should be included in the reformulation of the human rights conventions.

For over a millenium, Islamic law (Shari'a) gave women a more favorable status than the laws of many other traditions. Women were given greater protection in Islam than in other cultures. In the Islamic tradition, men have been regarded as the guardians of women. Muslims today, however, face some difficulties with human rights in the treatment of women and non-Muslims. Women receive only half a share in inheritance, and they receive less compensation than males in cases of criminal assault. Males may have four wives and divorce a wife at will, but women are allowed to have only one husband and to divorce only on very limited grounds. Women are generally not allowed as witnesses in serious criminal cases, and two women count for one witness in civil cases. Women are not allowed to hold public positions with authority over men. Non-Muslims must have special permission to practice their religion, they are excluded from positions of public authority, and they are subject to extra taxation.

Various nations, including the more developed, are violators of human rights. An-Na'im suggests that the concept of "essentially domestic jurisdiction" is a hindrance to the success of human rights. Sovereign states must work to bring the practices within their own jurisdiction into conformity with international law.

An-Na'im observes that the Western notion of rights is that rights are individual claims against the state. He notes that non-western notions of rights include economic and collective development. Rather than adopt an aggressive posture to impose a Western notion of rights, Western nations should examine their notion of rights and try to grasp the different perceptions of rights held in different parts of the world.

Each nation must probe and address its own violations of human rights and employ religious and other normative institutions to correct these violations. An-Na'im proposes that states work through local organizations, including religious and other normative institutions, to bring their practices in regard to human rights into conformity with the theory of human rights.

Native American Perspectives

Tecumseh

During the last decades of the 18th century, Tecumseh of the Shawnees witnessed broken treaties and the settlement of native hunting grounds by the Europeans. He actively encouraged various native American groups to unite and defend their lands against the encroachment of the European settlers. He described the attitude of Europeans toward native Americans: "The white men despise and cheat the Indians; they abuse and insult them; they do not think the red men sufficiently good to live."

Superior weaponry reinforced attitudes of political, social, and religious superiority on the part of Europeans. The deforestation of the land led to floods, and the hospitable reception of Europeans on the part of the native Americans was greeted with numerous acts of hostility. The Europeans' treatment of the land and of the natives prompted Tecumseh to declare that the Great Spirit was angry with the Europeans.

Vine Deloria

Vine Deloria challenges European-based scientific doctrines in his book *Red Earth, White Lies*. He raises critical doubts about claims of scientists that have the effect of placing native Americans in an unfavorable light. These views, in turn, serve to justify the subordinate social position assigned to native Americans by Europeans. The Bering Straits hypothesis, for example, makes native Americans relatively recent immigrants to the New World. It claims that Indians migrated across a land bridge between Asia and Alaska as recently as 12,000 years ago. This belief reinforces an AAE view that all humans had a single origin as described in the biblical account of creation. Deloria also finds that the hypothesis that big-game Indian hunters destroyed the fauna of the New World is an ironic distortion of the destructive abilities of bow and spear hunters.

Who can adopt a fair-minded perspective? Humans can be fair and choose how to relate to nature. Humans have the ability to decide whether to be part of nature or to stand apart from nature's way. The effort to adopt the timeless perspective on the part of native Americans, Vine Deloria may be interpreted as saying, was rejected on dogmatic grounds by members of the AAE tradition. Any viewpoint that did not correspond to the Christian religion was simply rejected. The clergy in the Christian tradition to which Vine Deloria refers reserved for themselves the role of fair-mindedness.

Why should the perspective of fairness be adopted? According to Deloria, a religious perspective that resembles the fairness perspective was adopted to protect life in all its forms—human and nonhuman, present and future generations. Not only animals, but all of nature should be represented from the timeless perspective. Deloria asserts that people who adopt a limited perspective–limited, that is, to a particular time or to the interests of specific individuals–suffer from a spiritual poverty. Decisions made from self-interest or even from sympathy are made from a limited perspective. The fair-minded perspective should be adopted so all creatures can be represented in the decisions made by humans.

Deloria holds that it is in the nature of religion "to exert a profound influence within societies and groups and sustain the community or national group over a period of time." Deloria's position does not view religion as offering speculative answers to the perennial questions. He belongs rather on the "practical reason" side of the communitarian school when he holds that "the Western world must be prepared to analyze religion as a phenomenon that does not necessarily explain the unanswered questions posed by the philosophical mind, but which may, in itself, cause such questions to occur to all manner of men in a great variety of situations." Without religion and its landmarks, Deloria maintains, national psychic stability is impossible.

Latin American Perspectives

Bartolome de Las Casas

Bartolome de Las Casas recounts the enslavement and destruction of native American populations by the Spanish in the 16th century. The

Spanish were seeking gold in the New World, according to Las Casas, and readily subjugated native populations to achieve this goal.

Augustinians would account for this treatment of non-Christians by saying that self-interest motivated the Spanish. Social disorder follows when people are motivated primarily by self-interest. One must probe further, however, and ask why Christian missionaries were unable–or even unwilling–to place restraints on their fellow countrymen's practices of enslavement. We have seen that followers of Augustine accepted the claim that only the few were capable of governing. Only some people, on this account, had the knowledge and the skill to rule the rest. The view that Christians had a superior religion was widely shared by Europeans, and this superior status allegedly entitled Europeans to rule over other peoples who lacked the military and political power to govern.

Gustavo Gutierrez

In answer to the question of whether the decision-making perspective is primarily communal or individual, Gustavo Gutierrez remarks that the individual does not form opinions in isolation. "We need not begin from scratch to work up our own private vision of reality." He favors the communal approach to decision-making, but in doing so he faces a difficulty: Which community makes the decisions? Different communities represent different perspectives.

Gutierrez addresses this problem by proposing that the perspective of those victimized by "institutional violence" is the viewpoint that can unite different communities. The community of Catholic religious leaders has been isolated from the community of the poor in Latin America. At different points in history, different circumstances contributed to this isolation. The first was a defensive stance that the Catholic Church took in opposition to other religions during the Counter-Reformation in the 16th and 17th centuries. In more recent centuries, the Catholic Church has sided with established authorities in response to attacks from liberal and anti-clerical groups.

Gutierrez responds to a document generated by the Catholic hierarchy of bishops in 1968, the Medellin document, in which the bishops expressed what they called a "preferential option for the poor." Gutierrez finds reason for hope that the bishops' preferential choice in favor of the poor may unite the community of the Catholic hierarchy with the community of the poor. The perspective for moral decision-making may become a single perspective in which the needs of the poor are taken into account. He calls on the bishops to recognize the implication that their preference for solidarity with the poor may involve giving up some of their own power. The bishops must declare their solidarity with the poor, Gutierrez maintains, "instead of what they have done in the past, when they have turned to those in power and called for necessary reforms while implying that their own position need not be affected by such change." A unity of the hierarchy with the poor would have the effect of inverting the social pyramid.

Who can achieve fair-mindedness? Everyone, whether rich or poor, can do so. Gutierrez presents solidarity with the poor and empowerment as virtues. He rejects a "hazy humanism" associated with liberalism and a "disembodied spiritualism" that is a remnant of religious dualism. An attitude of solidarity with the poor is a virtue among the clergy, and an attitude of empowerment is a virtue among the poor. When a preferential option for the poor comes to be expressed, the perspective of fairness will be employed. When fair-mindedness is present, the poor possess power. Hence, the poor must work to make their plight known. In such work lies virtue. In this way the poor come to possess "the power of the poor in history."

Why try to achieve fair-mindedness? Different communities can be united when the impartial, timeless perspective is adopted. In addition, according to Gutierrez, when the perspective of fairness is adopted, a new way to be human can be discovered. Gutierrez' approach has universal communitarian elements. He advocates more than a revolution; he envisions an order that will allow "a wholly new way for men and women to be human." Each unanimous decision from the impartial perspective that is made in response to slavery and colonialism defines a new way, in response to changing circumstances, to be human.

Why be careful in the quest for the fair, impartial perspective? Inverting the social pyramid and empowering the people can be a precarious enterprise. A timeless perspective has the potential for avoiding war and is adopted in part to achieve that end. The danger of civil war looms when the issues become sharp enough to prompt proposals to turn down the cards. The delicate balance between negotiation and war requires a deep commitment to justice from all sides if the balance is to be preserved.

Epilogue

The philosophers we have studied often found themselves in the midst of strife–social, political, and civil. As many other people have done in troubled times, philosophers have dreamt of a better world and shared their dreams with others.

We have studied some of the more influential utopian dreams or visions from the past. These visions of a better world have acted as powerful forces in human history. In recent centuries, the possibilities posed by the printing press and other means of disseminating information have fueled dreams of universal literacy and democratic government. Utopian visions of freedom from the indignity of slavery and the drudgery of manual labor have stimulated the development of industry and technology. In industrial societies, the development of money rather than land as the measure of wealth has fired the imaginations of egalitarian thinkers who have proposed a redistribution of wealth to bring an end to class division. So powerful are these visions of human betterment, however, that many who share them have neglected a negative underside that accompanies the pursuit of such grand visions.

Rights that protect people from slavery, genocide and religious persecution have emerged following wars in recent centuries. Persons committed to human rights and a fair social game may ask whether rights can be created prior to the outbreak of war. The potential for tyranny in various forms may be reduced if early alarms are heeded.

Voices have been raised that warn against the negative side of the pursuit of the betterment of humanity. A student of mine from Sierra Leone has commented, "The U.S. is a good country, but it needs help." Help may be available from societies that, unlike the European, have not engaged in widespread colonization when social problems have arisen. Some societies whose members have stayed at home and tried to work out social problems have developed moral and political philosophies that could help to detect early warnings of difficulties for the United States and other industrial societies.

The early warning system in the United States includes the voices of women and minorities within the U.S. who have suffered from oppressive policies. These voices have for the most part been practical in their social philosophies. When these voices are heard, experiments in democracy and industrialization seem more likely to succeed. A failure to heed these voices, as history has shown, may lead such social experiments to collapse into chaos and civil war.

One of the early alarms expressed by some feminist, minority, and multicultural voices is the threat to the nurturing of the next generation. When a culture destroys that relationship by destroying families, for example, important boundaries have been overstepped. Marketplace forces can overwhelm and destroy families, and when the values of the marketplace are given priority in a culture the threat to the family may be extensive. The destruction of the slave family in the U.S. lay at the core of the tyranny associated with chattel slavery. The destruction of the food supply of native Americans threatened the survival of families and exposed a genocidal policy.

Other early warning signals have also appeared. The voices of descendants of chattel slaves have made clear the inhumanity and horror of reducing persons to mere property. The realization that some Euro-Americans were capable of relating to other persons as mere things serves as an urgent reminder that vigilance and reform are necessary to prevent new forms of slavery—perhaps in the form of class division fed by slave wages.

A related warning is that resentment accompanies class division. Europeans have had a tradition of class division based on land ownership. Although many people have envisioned a new day of more equal distribution of social goods made possible since money rather than land has become the measure of wealth, money seems to be simply replacing land as a basis for class division. The warning from past class revolts and civil wars is that resentment over class division can collapse a society.

Warnings that money can become destructive may also be heard in various quarters. Some branches of Islam warn against the use of money to make money—that is, against the practice of paying and collecting interest. Society can deteriorate into two classes when interest is used as a means of making money. Society can become divided into those who mainly collect interest and those who mainly pay it. When the practice of interest is combined with the pursuit of maximum profits, the warning signals become rather clear. The profit motive during the slave era became so intoxicating that many were blinded to the inhumanity of slavery. Native American voices also caution against reducing the land to mere monetary value.

The Nazi holocaust and other instances of ethnic hatred sound harsh warnings to the AAE tradition. Efforts to increase human welfare are likely to be accompanied by preferences for specific notions of a good life. When philosophers and other leaders espouse a notion of the good life that rests on a rejection of the other–the foreigner, the stranger, those allegedly governed in a patriarchal or tribal fashion–the effect can snowball into civil and social disasters. These exclusionary attitudes may indicate that people have become intoxicated with a particular way of life.

The Hindu tradition provides a reminder that class division requires the acceptance of a shared notion of life's purpose. A caste system can be stable if its members accept a shared notion of the good life. In the absence of a shared notion of the purpose or meaning of life, however, some people inevitably impose their own notion of the good life on others when a division between classes is present. Arbitrary treatment of some people by others can result. To avoid this form of tyranny, the liberal tradition has proposed that the individual should determine the good or meaningful life. If a liberal democracy with a free market economy moves toward class division based on income and monetary wealth, the warning from Hinduism is that social instability can result unless a shared notion of life's purpose is found. In short, a democratic society may be forced to choose between two nearly irreconcilable alternatives: liberal equality on the one hand and a free market with its class divisions on the other. Efforts to include both could render the society unstable.

The voices of successful non-violent political movements–led by Desmond Tutu in South Africa, Mahatma Gandhi in India, and Martin Luther King in the United States–provide a reminder that the fairminded, cards-down perspective can sometimes be adopted before war breaks out.

A public voice for women has only gradually and partially been won. The exclusion of women from voting, education, and property ownership–even during periods of widespread literacy and industrialization–is a warning that human rights can be unevenly and unequally distributed. The shift from agricultural, land-based economies to money-based economies has fueled dreams of more equal distribution of income between males and females, but these dreams have been only partially realized.

Several issues have emerged from our study: Can social life be played as a fair game? Can people negotiate rights, or must rights be won through violence? Can early warning signs of oppression be heeded and rights created in advance of war and civil chaos, or do people realize that the social game has become unfair only after the game has collapsed into violent conflict?

The main question of the philosophers we have studied has been how to bring about a fair social game. Some have said fairness can be directly attained by viewing social life as a rule-governed game, and from this practical perspective morality and justice can be achieved. For this group of practical thinkers, people's ordinary intuitions and judgments provide adequate grounds for determining fairness. Others have taken a more speculative approach and said that, if stability is to be attained, a world view or a religion must support morality and justice. Both groups of philosophers–even the speculative thinkers– view themselves as participants in the practice of creating a fair social game. The speculative group hopes to contribute to solutions to moral and political issues by providing more accurate accounts of what is real and true.

As both spectators and players in the social game, philosophers have found different motives at work. Each philosophical theory or picture of morality we have examined has proposed a place for self-interest, altruism, and fair-mindedness. Several factors have contributed to a growing conviction that all persons, not just the few, are capable of fair-mindedness. Each person and culture, according to this vision, can contribute to the creation of social life as a fair game.

A common theme has emerged from the various philosophies we have studied: humans regard a fair game of life worth playing, so a fair social game is worth working to achieve. To borrow an expression from Gustavo Gutierrez, each time the cards have gone down and an impartial view has been adopted toward oppressive practices–slavery, segregation, colonialism, religious intolerance, and the denial of a public voice to women and minorities–a new way of being human has emerged. Since slavery, religious intolerance, patriarchy, and colonialism can take new forms, each generation increases the chances of balancing conflicting values by remaining vigilant and heeding the cries of those who suffer oppression.

Bibliographical Notes

Chapter 1: Some Preliminaries

Ronald Green, "The Rawls Game," *Teaching Philosophy*, 9:1 (March 1986): 51-60. Phillip Montague's refutation of relativism appears in "Are There Objective and Absolute Moral Standards?" in *Reason and Responsibility*, ed. Joel Feinberg (Belmont, CA: Wadsworth, 1978).

Chapter 2: Ancient and Medieval Moral Communitarianism

Plato. See *The Republic of Plato*, tr. Francis MacDonald Cornford (New York: Oxford University Press, 1945); *The Dialogues of Plato*, in two volumes, tr. B. Jowett (New York: Macmillan, Random House, 1892).

For commentary and interpretation, see *Great Thinkers on Plato*, ed. Barry Gross (New York: Capricorn Books, 1969); *Plato: A Collection of Critical Essays*, in two volumes, ed. Gregory Vlastos (Garden City, N.Y.: Doubleday, Anchor Books, 1971).

Augustine. St. Augustine, *The City of God* (New York: Random House, The Modern Library, 1950); *The Confessions of St. Augustine*, tr. F. J. Sheed (New York: Sheed and Ward, 1943); *Augustine: Political Writings*, tr. Michael W. Tkacz and Douglas Kries (Indianapolis, IN: Hackett Publishing Co., 1994).

For commentary and interpretation, see Karl Jaspers, *Plato and Augustine: from The Great Philosophers, Vol. 1*, ed. Hannah Arendt (New York: Harcourt, Brace and World, Inc., 1962), pp. 102-119.

Aristotle. *Nichomachean Ethics: Aristotle*, tr. Martin Ostwald (Indianapolis, IN: Bobbs-Merrill, 1962); Aristotle's criticisms of Plato's ideal state are drawn from his *Politics*, Book II, in *The Basic Works of Aristotle*, ed. Richard McKeon (New York: Random House, 1941). A highly accessible account is given by Mortimer J. Adler in *Aristotle for Everybody: Difficult Thought Made Easy* (New York: Macmillan, Bantam Book, 1978). For an account of Aristotelian perfectionism as part of the backdrop of modern-day racism see Lucius T. Outlaw, Jr., *On Race and Philosophy* (New York: Routledge, 1996), pp. 192-194. I owe the notion of organizational structures as upright or inverted pyramids to my professor Charles Curran at the Catholic University of America, Washington, DC.

Aquinas. Thomas Aquinas, *Treatise on Man: St. Thomas Aquinas*, tr. James F. Anderson (Englewood Cliffs, N.J.: Prentice-Hall, Inc., 1962); *The Political Ideas of St. Thomas Aquinas*, ed. Dino Bigongiari (New York: Hafner Press, 1953); *Summa Contra Gentiles* and *Summa Theologica*, ed. A. C. Pegis (New York: Random House, The Modern Library, 1945).

For commentary and interpretation of Aquinas, see Jacques Maritain, *Existence and the Existent: An Essay on Christian Existentialism*, tr. Lewis Galantiere and Gerald B. Phelan (New York: Doubleday, Image Book, 1948).

Chapter 3: Roots of Modern Moral Liberalism
    Epicurus. For further reading, see *Epicurus: The Extant Remains*, tr. Cyril Bailey (Oxford, Clarendon Press, 1926).
    For commentary and interpretation, see Lucretius, *On the Nature of the Universe*, Baltimore: Penguin Classics, 1951.
    Epictetus. On Epictetus, see *Handbook of Epictetus*, tr. Nicholas White, (Indianapolis, IN: Hackett Publishing Co., 1983).
    For commentary and interpretation, see Brad Inwood, *Ethics and Human Action in Early Stoicism* (New York: Oxord, Clarendon Press, 1985).
    Maimonides. The source for the discussion of Maimonides is *Guide for the Perplexed*, tr. M. Friedlander (London: Routledge and Sons, 1904).
    For commentary and interpretation, see Idit Dobbs-Weinstein, *Maimonides and St Thomas on the Limits of Reason* (Albany: State University of New York Press, 1995).
    Hobbes. Hobbes' main work on moral and political philosophy is *Leviathan* (1651). It has been published in 1985 in the Penguin Classics series and edited by C. B. MacPherson.
    For commentary and interpretation, see Michael Walzer, "The Communitarian Critique of Liberalism," *Political Theory*, 18 (1), (February 1990): 6-23.
    Hume. Hume's works on moral and political philosophy include *A Treatise of Human Nature* (1739), *An Enquiry Concerning the Principles of Morals* (1748), and *Essays, Moral and Political* (1741-1742). These works appear in *Hume's Moral and Political Philosophy*, ed. Henry D. Aiken (New York: Hafner Press, 1948). His discussion of the social contract is the subject of his essay, "Of the Original Contract," which is Chapter IX of *Essays, Moral and Political*. He discusses self-interest (self-love) in Appendix II of *An Enquiry Concerning the Principles of Morals*.

Chapter 4: Modern Moral Liberalism
    Locke and Jefferson. The material on Locke is drawn from his *Second Treatise of Government*, Chapters II through IX. For Jefferson's comments on the Platonisms grafted onto Christianity, see his letter to John Adams, July 5, 1814, quoted in *Jefferson Himself*, ed. Bernard Mayo (Charlottesville, VA: The University Press of Virginia, 1942), pp. 300-301. The discussion of Jefferson is drawn in part from Fawn M. Brodie, *Thomas Jefferson: An Intimate History* (New York: W.W. Norton & Co., 1974). The response to his Virginia peers in the matter of miscegenation is presented on p. 391 of Brodie, and his opinion on whether blacks and whites can live under the same government is cited on p. 441. The quotation in which Jefferson refers to the degradation that results from miscegenation appears in Jefferson's letter to Edward Coles, August 25, 1814. A contemporary Lockean position is outlined in Robert Nozick, *Anarchy, State, and Utopia* (New York: Basic Books, Inc., 1974). Another

contemporary who echoes a Lockean version of libertarianism is John Hospers, "What Libertarianism Is," in *Liberty for the Twenty-First Century: Contemporary Libertarian Thought*, ed. Tibor R. Machan (Lanham, MD: Rowman & Littlefield, 1995).

Kant. The discussion of Kant's moral and political philosophy is drawn mainly from *Fundamental Principles of the Metaphysic of Morals*, tr. Thomas K. Abbott (New York: The Liberal Arts Press, 1949); *Critique of Practical Reason*, (1788), tr. Lewis White Beck (Indianapolis, IN: Bobbs-Merrill, 1956); *The Metaphysical Elements of Justice*, (1797) tr. John Ladd, (Indianapolis, IN: Bobbs-Merrill, 1965); and *Eternal Peace*, (1795) tr. Carl J. Friedrich, in *The Philosophy of Kant: Immanuel Kant's Moral and Political Writings* (New York: Random House, The Modern Library, 1949), pp. 430-476; Kant's comments on Africans may be found in his essay "Observations on the Feeling of the Beautiful and Sublime," tr. John T. Goldthwait (Berkeley: University of California Press, 1960), pp. 110-114; Kant's remarks about the village and the nomadic ways of life may be found in "Conjectural Beginning of Human History," tr. Emil L. Fackenheim, in *Kant On History* (Indianapolis: Bobbs-Merrill, 1963).

For commentary and interpretation, see Bruce Aune, *Kant's Theory of Morals* (Princeton, N.J.: Princeton University Press, 1979); Lewis White Beck, *A Commentary on Kant's Critique of Practical Reason* (Chicago: University of Chicago Press, 1960); Robert Paul Wolff, *The Autonomy of Reason: A Commentary on Kant's Groundwork of the Metaphysic of Morals* (New York: Harper and Row, 1973); Marcus G. Singer, "Reconstructing the *Groundwork*," *Ethics*, 93 (April 1983): 566-578.

Bentham. My discussion of Bentham is drawn from *The Principles of Morals and Legislation* (New York: Hafner Press, 1948).

For commentary and interpretation, see John Stuart Mill, "Bentham," in *The Six Great Humanistic Essays of John Stuart Mill* (New York: Washington Square Press, 1963)., pp. 27-70.

Mill and Taylor. In his dedication to *On Liberty*, John Stuart Mill refers to Harriet Taylor as "the inspirer, and in part the author, of all that is best in my writings." The main sources of their work are "Utilitarianism," pp. 243-308 in *The Six Great Humanistic Essays of John Stuart Mill* (New York: Washington Square Press, 1963); and *On Liberty*, ed. Alburey Castell, New York: Appleton-Century-Crofts, 1947).

For commentary and interpretation, see Richard B. Brandt, "The Real and Alleged Problems of Utilitarianism," *Hastings Center Report*,13 (April 1983): 37-43; J. J. C. Smart and Bernard Williams, *Utilitarianism: For and Against* (London: Cambridge University Press, 1973).

Marx. The main sources for the discussion of Marx are *The Communist Manifesto* and *Criticism of the Gotha Program*, which appear in Karl Marx, *Capital* (New York: The Modern Library, 1932).

For commentary and interpretation, see Michael Walzer, "The Communitarian Critique of Liberalism," *Political Theory*, 18:1 (February 1990): 6-23.

Rawls. The main sources of Rawls' material are *A Theory of Justice* (Cambridge, Mass.: The Belknap Press of the Harvard University Press, 1971); and·*Political Liberalism* (New York: Columbia University Press, 1993). For commentary and interpretation, see Robert Paul Wolff, *Understanding Rawls* (Princeton, N.J.: Princeton University Press, 1977). Stephen Mulhall and Adam Swift provide a summary of communitarian criticisms of Rawls in *Liberals and Communitarians* (Cambridge, Mass.: Blackwell, 1992).

Beauvoir and Sartre. The main sources of Simone de Beauvoir's thought are *The Second Sex,* translated and edited by H. M. Parshley (New York: Alfred A. Knopf Bantam Book, 1952); and *The Ethics of Ambiguity*, tr. Bernard Prechtman (New York: Citadel Press, 1964). Sartre presents a central theme of his philosophy in the chapter "My Death" in *Being and Nothingness* (New York: Washington Square Press, 1966), pp. 680-707. A good brief introduction to Sartre's philosophy is the essay "Existentialism," in *Existentialism and Human Emotions* (New York: Philosophical Library, 1957), pp. 9-51.

Chapter 5: Contemporary Communitarianism

MacIntyre. The discussion of Alasdair MacIntyre draws upon *After Virtue* (Notre Dame, IN: University of Notre Dame Press, 1984) particularly chapter twelve, "Aristotle's Account of the Virtues."

For commentary and interpretation, see the criticisms of MacIntyre in *After MacIntyre*, ed. John Horton and Susan Mendus (Notre Dame, IN: University of Notre Dame Press, 1994). MacIntyre responds to several critics in the final article of the book, "A Partial Response to My Critics."

Sandel. Sandel discusses the three conceptions of community on pages 147-161 of *Liberalism and the Limits of Justice* (Cambridge: Cambridge University Press, 1970).

For commentary and interpretation, see Chapter One in Stephen Mulhall and Adam Swift, *Liberals and Communitarians* (Cambridge, Mass: Blackwell, 1992).

Charles Taylor. The material on Taylor draws upon "Kant's Theory of Freedom," chapter twelve of Charles Taylor, *Philosophical Papers 2: Philosophy and the Human Sciences* (Cambridge University Press, 1985); and his essay "Atomism," in *Powers, Possessions, and Freedom*, ed. Alkis Kontos (Toronto: University of Toronto Press, 1979), pp. 39-62.

For commentary and interpretation, see Chapter Three in Stephen Mulhall and Adam Swift, *Liberals and Communitarians* (Cambridge, Mass: Blackwell, 1992).

Mussolini. Benito Mussolini, *Fascism: Doctrines and Institutions* (New York: Howard Fertig, 1968).

King. The discussion of M. L. King draws upon his "Letter from Birmingham Jail," from *Why We Can't Wait* (New York: Harper and Row, 1963), pp.77-100; reprinted in *The Norton Anthology of African American Literature*, ed. Henry Louis Gates, Jr. and Nellie Y. McKay (New York: W. W. Norton and Co., 1997).

For commentary and interpretation, see "In Pursuit of a Just Society: Martin Luther King, Jr, and John Rawls," by Robert M. Franklin, *Journal of Religious Ethics*, 18:2 (Fall 1990): 57-77.

West. The material from Cornel West is drawn from *Race Matters* by Cornel West (New York: Random House Vintage Books, 1990); and his article, "Philosophy, Politics, and Power: An Afro-American Perspective," in *Philosophy Born of Struggle*, ed. Leonard Harris (Kendall/Hunt Publishing Co., 1983).

For commentary and interpretation, see "Cornel West as Pragmatist and Existentialist" by Clarence Shole Johnson, in *Existence in Black: An Anthology of Black Existential Philosophy*, ed. Lewis R. Gordon (New York: Routledge, 1997).

Lawson. Lawson's argument on African-Americans and a state of nature appears in "Citizenship and Slavery," chapter four of *Between Slavery and Freedom: Philosophy and American Slavery*, by Howard McGary and Bill E. Lawson (Bloomington, Ind.: Indiana University Press, 1992). The material by Harvey Natanson is from his article "Locke and Hume: Bearing on the Legal Obligation of the Negro," *Journal of Value Inquiry* 5:1 (1970): 35-43.

Outlaw. Lucius Outlaw, *On Race and Philosophy* (New York: Routledge, 1996), pp. 43-49, 192-204; Arthur Lovejoy, *The Great Chain of Being* (Cambridge, MA: Harvard University Press, 1961). Statements on race by Hume, Kant, Hegel, and Jefferson may be found in *Race and the Enlightenment*, ed. Emmanuel Chukwuki Eze (Malden, MA: Blackwell Publishers, 1997).

Baier. The discussion of Annette Baier draws upon her article "Trust and Antitrust," *Ethics*, 96 (January 1986): 231-260. Another helpful article for understanding Baier's position is her article "What Do Women Want in a Moral Theory?" *Nous*, 19 (March 1985), reprinted in Kittay, E. and Meyers, D., eds., *Women and Moral Theory* (Totowa, N.J.: Rowman and Littlefield, 1987). For commentary and interpretation, see "Response to My Critics," by Annette Baier in *Hume Studies*, 20:2 (November 1994): 211-218, where she identifies and responds to several criticisms of her position.

Ruddick. Sara Ruddick, "Maternal Thinking," *Feminist Studies*, 6 (Summer 1980): 342-367; *Maternal Thinking: Toward a Politics of Peace*, (Boston: Beacon Press, 1989).

Grimshaw. Jean Grimshaw, "The Idea of a Female Ethic," in *A Companion to Ethics*, ed. Peter Singer (Oxford: Blackwell, 1991), pp. 491-499, reprinted in James Rachels, *The Right Thing To Do*, 2nd ed. (New York: McGraw-Hill, 1999), pp. 83-94.

Chapter 6: Metaphysics

Democritus. Most of our knowledge of Democritus' writings comes from later authors. Aristotle describes the position of Democritus in *Metaphysics, Physics, On the Heavens, On the Soul,* and *On the Generation of Animals.* A concise summary of Aristotle's and other sources may be found in Chapter Six of *The Presocratics,* ed. Philip Wheelwright (Indianapolis, IN: Bobbs-Merrill, The Odyssey Press, 1966).

For commentary and interpretation, see Aristotle, *On Generation and Corruption,* 316a-b, *Physics* 231a, and *On the Heavens* 303a.

Pythagoras. See chapter seven of *The Presocratics,* ed. Philip Wheelwright (Indianapolis, IN: Bobbs-Merrill, The Odyssey Press, 1966).

Parmenides. See chapter four of *The Presocratics,* ed. Philip Wheelwright (Indianapolis, IN: Bobbs-Merrill, The Odyssey Press, 1966).

Plato. Plato's doctrine of the Forms may be found in Sections 509-534 of Plato's *Republic.* Also see the dialogues *Symposium, Phaedo,* and *Timaeus.*

For commentary and interpretation, see *Great Thinkers on Plato,* ed. Barry Gross (New York: Capricorn Books, 1969); *Plato: A Collection of Critical Essays,* in two volumes, ed. Gregory Vlastos (Garden City, N.Y.: Doubleday, Anchor Books, 1971).

Aristotle. A highly readable account of Aristotle's views for introductory students may be found in Mortimer J.Adler, *Aristotle for Everybody: Difficult Thought Made Easy* (New York: Macmillan, Bantam Book, 1978).

For commentary and criticism, see Alasdair MacIntyre, "Virtues, Unity of Life, and Concept of a Tradition," Chapter 15 in *After Virtue,* 2nd ed., (Notre Dame, IN: University of Notre Dame Press, 1984).

Kant. Kant's discussion of the antinomies of reason may be found in his *Critique of Pure Reason,* tr. Norman Kemp Smith (New York: St. Martin's Press, 1965_, pp. 393-421 (1929 edition of Macmillan, 426-460). One of Kant's central discussions of freedom is found in the third section of his *Fundamental Principles of the Metaphysic of Morals* (New York: The Liberal Arts Press, 1949). Also see his *Critique of Practical Reason,* tr. Lewis White Beck (Indianapolis, IN: Bobbs-Merrill, The Library of Liberal Arts, 1956).

For commentary and interpretation, see Karl Ameriks, "Kant," in *The Cambridge Dictionary of Philosophy,* ed. Robert Audi (Cambridge, UK: Cambridge University Press, 1995_, pp. 398-403; Norman Kemp Smith, *A Commentary to Kant's Critique of Pure Reason* (Humanities Press, 1991).

Chapter 7: Epistemology
Theories of Truth. Richard L. Kirkham, *Theories of Truth: A Critical Introduction* (Cambridge, MA: The MIT Press, A Bradford Book, 1992); William James, "Pragmatism's Conception of Truth," in *Essays in Pragmatism* (New York: Hafner Publ. Co., 1969); Thomas Kuhn, *The Structure of Scientific Revolutions* (Chicago: University of Chicago Press, 1970).

Knowledge: Theories of Justification. See Louis P. Pojman, ed., *The Theory of Knowledge: Classic and Contemporary Readings* (Belmont, CA: Wadsworth Publishing Co., 1993); for a discussion of the distinction between giving a representation of the world and dealing with the world, see Charles Taylor, "Overcoming Epistemology," Chapter One in *Philosophical Arguments* (Cambridge, MA: Harvard University Press, 1995); Carnegie's comments may be found in the *Autobiography of Andrew Carnegie* (Boston, 1920), p. 327.

Foundationalism. Rene Descartes, *Discourse on Method and The Meditations Concerning First Philosophy* (Indianapolis, IN: Bobbs-Merrill, Liberal Arts Press, 1960); Thomas Hobbes, *Leviathan* (1651), (New York: Penguin Books, 1968), Chapter IX.

Emergence of anti-foundationalism. *Anti-foundationalism: Old and New*, ed. Tom Rockmore and Beth Singer (Philadelphia: Temple University Press, 1992); Lawrence Bonjour, "A Critique of Foundationalism," in *The Theory of Knowledge: Classic and Contemporary Readings*, ed. Louis P. Pojman (Belmont, CA: Wadsworth Publishing Co., 1993), pp. 214-225; Alasdair MacIntyre, *Whose Justice? Which Rationality?* (Notre Dame, IN: University of Notre Dame Press, 1988); John Rawls aligned with Kant's moral philosophy in *A Theory of Justice* (Cambridge, MA: Harvard University Press, 1971), but in *Political Liberalism* (New York: Columbia University Press, 1993), Rawls claimed neutrality on all "comprehensive doctrines"–that is, moral, religious, epistemological, and metaphysical doctrines.

Otto Neurath, "Foundations of the Social Sciences," Chapter One in *Foundations of the Unity of Science*, Vol. II, ed. Otto Neurath, Rudolf Carnap, and Charles Morris (Chicago: The University of Chicago Press [original edition, 1939], 1970), pp. 1-47; Ernest Sosa, "The Raft and the Pyramid: Coherence versus Foundations in the Theory of Knowledge," in *The Theory of Knowledge: Classic and Contemporary Readings*, ed. Louis P. Pojman (Wadsworth, 1993), pp. 246-262.

Richard Kirkham comments on Peirce's theory in *Theories of Truth* (Cambridge, MA: The MIT Press, 1992), p. 83; John Dewey, *The Quest for Certainty*, 1929, (New York: Capricorn Books, 1960).

George Edward Moore, *Principia Ethica*, 1903 (Cambridge: Cambridge University Press, 1959); Alfred Jules Ayer, *Language, Truth, and Logic* (Harmondsworth, Middlesex, Eng., Penguin Books, 1971); R. M. Hare, *The Language of Morals* (New York: Oxford University Press, 1964); Ludwig Wittgenstein, *On Certainty* (New York: Harper Collins, 1986); *Tractatus*

Logico-Philosophicus, tr. C.K. Ogden and F.P. Ramsey (London: Kegal Paul, 1922).

Chapter 8: The Existence of God

Descartes. Rene Descartes, *The Meditations Concerning the First Philosophy*, III (Indianapolis: Bobbs-Merrill, The Library of Liberal Arts, 1960), pp. 91-107; *Anselm of Canterbury*, Vol. 1, ed. Jasper Hopkins and Herbert Richardson (Toronto: The Edwin Mellen Press, 1974).

For commentary and criticism, see Immanuel Kant, *Critique of Pure Reason*, tr. Norman Kemp Smith, New York: St. Martin's Press, 1965), pp. 500-507; also Kant's *Religion Within the Limits of Reason Alone*, tr. Theodore M. Greene and Hoyt H. Hudson (New York: Harper and Row, Harper Torchbooks, 1960); Charles Hartshorne, "The Necessarily Existent," in *The Ontological Argument*, ed. Alvin Plantinga (New York: Doubleday Anchor Books, 1965), pp. 123-135.

Pascal. Blaise Pascal, *Pensees*, tr. W. Trotter (London: Dent & Co., 1908).

James. William James, "The Will to Believe" and "Is Life Worth Living?" in *The Will To Believe and Other Essays in Popular Philosophy*, (New York: Longmans, Green and Co., 1923), pp. 1-62; *The Varieties of Religious Experience: A Study in Human Nature* (New York: Longmans, Green and Co., 1902).

Aquinas. For Aquinas' presentation of proofs for the existence of God, see *Summa Theologica*, I, question 2, in *Introduction to Saint Thomas Aquinas*, ed. Anton C. Pegis (New York: Random House, The Modern Library, 1948).

For commentary and interpretation, see Etienne Gilson, *God and Philosophy* (New Haven: Yale University Press, 1941).

Walker. Preamble and Article 1 of *David Walker's Appeal in Four Articles; Together with a Preamble, to the Coloured Citizens of the World*, reprinted in *The Norton Anthology of African American Literature*, ed. Henry Louis Gates, Jr. and Nellie Y. McKay (New York: W. W. Norton and Company, 1997), pp. 179-189. The distinction between the "forth-telling" and "fore-telling" roles of prophesy is drawn from Roland Murphy, my scripture professor at the Catholic University of America, Washington, DC.

Chapter 9: Feminist Perspectives

Several of the articles summarized in this chapter on feminist perspectives and in the next chapter on multicultural perspectives appear in *Social and Political Philosophy: Classical Western Texts in Feminist and Multicultural Perspectives*, 2nd ed., ed. James Sterba (Belmont, CA: Wadsworth Publishing Company, 1998).

On Plato. Lynda Lange, "The Function of Equal Education in Plato's *Republic* and *Laws*," reprinted in *Social and Political Philosophy: Classical Western Texts in Feminist and Multicultural Perspectives*, 2nd ed., ed. James Sterba (Belmont, CA: Wadsworth Publishing Company, 1998), pp. 34-41, with acknowledgement to the University of Toronto Press; Susan Moller Okin, "Philosopher Queens and Private Wives: Plato on Women and the Family," in *The Family in Political Thought*, ed. Jean Bethke Elshtain (Amherst: The University of Massachusetts Press, 1982), pp. 31-50.

On Aristotle. Jean Bethke Elshtain, "Aristotle, the Public-Private Split, and the Case of the Suffragists," in *The Family in Political Thought*, ed. Jean Bethke Elshtain (Amherst: The University of Massachusetts Press, 1982), pp. 51-65; Elizabeth V. Spelman, "Aristotle and the Politicization of the Soul," in *Discovering Reality*, ed. S. Harding (Dordrecht: Reidel, Kluwer Academic Publishers, 1983), reprinted in Sterba, pp. 74-83.

On Augustine. Rosemary Radford Ruether, "Misogynism and Virginal Feminism in the Fathers of the Church," from *Religion and Sexism* ed. Rosemary Radford Ruether, reprinted in *Woman in Western Thought*, ed. Martha Lee Osborne (New York: Random House, 1979), pp. 62-65.

On Hobbes. Carole Pateman's article appears in "Hobbes, Patriarchy, and Conjugal Right," reprinted in Sterba, pp. 152-165 with permission of the author acknowledged.

On Locke. Lorenne M. G. Clark, "Women and John Locke; or, Who Owns the Apples in the Garden of Eden?" *The Canadian Journal of Philosophy*, 7 (December 1977): 699-724, reprinted in Sterba, pp. 193-209; Mary Lyndon Shanley, "Marriage Contract and Social Contract in Seventeenth-Century English Political Thought," in *The Family in Political Thought*, ed. Jean Bethke Elshtain (Amherst: The University of Massachusetts Press, 1982), pp. 80-95.

On Kant. Susan Mendus, "Kant: An Honest but Narrow-Minded Bourgeois?" in *Women in Western Political Philosophy*, ed. Ellen Kennedy and Susan Mendus (St. Martin's Press, 1987), reprinted in Sterba, pp. 289-300.

On Mill. Mary Lyndon Shanley, "Marital Slavery and Friendship: John Stuart Mill's *The Subjection of Women*," *Political Theory*, 9 (May 1981): 229-247, reprinted in Sterba, pp. 344-355.

On Marx. Heidi Hartmann, "The Unhappy Marriage Between Marxism and Feminism: Toward a More Progressive Union," reprinted in Sterba, pp. 384-394, with acknowledgement to the South End Press; Jane Humphries, "The Working Class Family: A Marxist Perspective," in *The Family in Political Thought*, ed. Jean Bethke Elshtain (Amherst: The University of Massachusetts Press, 1982), pp. 197-222.

On Rawls. "Justice as Fairness–For Whom?" in Susan Moller Okin, *Justice, Gender and the Family* (Harper Collins Publishers, Basic Books, 1989), reprinted in Sterba, pp. 444-456.

On MacIntyre. Elizabeth Frazer and Nicola Lacey, "MacIntyre, Feminism and the Concept of Practice," in *After MacIntyre*, ed. John Horton and Susan Mendus (South Bend, IN: University of Notre Dame Press, 1994), pp. 265-282; Marilyn Friedman, "Feminism and Modern Friendship: Dislocating the

Community," *Ethics*, 99 (January 1989): 275-290, reprinted in Sterba, pp. 530-540.

Chapter 10:: Multicultural Perspectives

Confucianist. A description of filial piety and the mandate of heaven, or dynàstic mandate, may be found in *Sources of Chinese Tradition*, Vol. 1, ed. Wm. Theodore de Bary et al. (New York: Columbia University Press, 1960), pp. 169-182. The views of Mencius and Hsun Tzu on human nature are presented in the same volume. The Japanese Ministry of Education's position on filial piety is found in *Fundamentals of Our National Polity*, 1937, reprinted in *Sources of Japanese Tradition*, Vol. 2, ed. Wm. Theodore de Bary et al. (New York: Columbia University Press, 1958).

Buddhist. *Buddhism: The Dhammapadha*, tr. John Ross Carter and Mahinda Palihawadana, Vol. 6 of *Sacred Writings*, ed. Jaroslav Pelikan, (New York: Oxford University Press, Quality Paperback Book Club, 1987); E. F. Schumacher, *Small Is Beautiful: Economics as if People Mattered*, (Harper Collins, 1973), excerpted, *Social and Political Philosophy: Classical Western Texts in Feminist and Multicultural Perspectives*, 2nd ed., ed. James Sterba (Belmont, CA: Wadsworth Publishing Company, 1998), pp. 395-400.

Hindu. Sarvepelli Radhakrishnan, *An Idealist View of Life* (London: George Allen & Unwin, 1932), pp. 218-223, reprinted in *Voices of Wisdom*, ed. Gary E. Kessler (Belmont, CA: Wadsworth Publ. Co., 1992), pp. 213-216; Mahatma K. Gandhi, "On Satyagraha," reprinted in James Sterba, *Social and Political Philosophy: Classical Western Texts in Feminist and Multicultural Perspectives*, 2nd ed. (Belmont, CA: Wadsworth, 1998), pp. 301-305, with acknowledgement to the Oxford University Press; S. E. Frost, Jr., ed., *The Sacred Writings of the World's Great Religions*, Chapter One: "Hinduism: The Rig-Veda, The Upanishads, The Bhagavad-Gita," (New York: McGraw-Hill, 1972); Stephen H. Phillips, "South Asian Philosophy," in *World Philosophy: A Text with Readings*, ed. Robert C. Solomon and Kathleen Higgins (New York: McGraw-Hill, 1995), pp. 65-119.

African. Chinua Achebe, *Things Fall Apart* (New York: Doubleday, Anchor Book, 1959); Chinwe Okechukwu, *The Predicament* (Kutztown, PA: Diaspora Publ., 1998); Frantz Fanon, *The Wretched of the Earth*, tr. Constance Farrington (New York: Grove Press, 1963); Desmond Tutu, *Crying In the Wilderness: A Struggle for Justice in South Africa*, (A.R. Mowbray and Co., 1990). An account of Igbo forms of government may be found in Chapter 4 of Victor C. Uchendu, *The Igbo of Southeast Nigeria*, (New York: Holt, Rinehart and Winston, 1965

Islamic. Abdullah Ahmed An-Na'im, "Islam, Islamic Law, and the Dilemma of Cultural Legitimacy for Universal Human Rights," Claude E. Welch and Virginia Leary, ed., *Asian Perspectives on Human Rights*, (Boulder, CO: Westview Press, 1990), reprinted in Larry May *et al.*, ed. *Applied Ethics*, (Upper Saddle River, NJ: Prentice Hall, 1994).

Abu'l A'la Mawdudi, "Political Theory of Islam," from *The Islamic Law and Constitution*, in *Voices of Wisdom: A Multicultural Philosophy Reader*, ed. Gary E. Kessler (Belmont, CA: Wadsworth, 1992), pp. 120-128; *The Sacred Writings of the World's Great Religions*, Selections from the *Koran*, ed. S. E. Frost, Jr. (New York: McGraw Hill, 1972), pp. 307-345.

Native American. Tecumseh, "We Must Be United," from John D. Hunter, *Memoirs of a Captivity Among the Indians of North America*, (London, 1824), reprinted in *Social and Political Philosophy*, 2nd ed., ed. James Sterba (Belmont, CA: Wadsworth, 1998), pp. 210-211; Vine Deloria, Jr., *God Is Red*, selections reprinted in Brooke Noel Moore and Kenneth Bruder, *Philosophy: The Power of Ideas*, 3rd ed., (Mountain View, CA: Mayfield, 1996), pp. 672-674, with acknowledgement to Fulcrum Publishing; Vine Deloria, Jr., *Red Earth, White Lies* (Golden, CO: Fulcrum Publishing, 1997).

Latin American. Gustavo Gutierrez, from *The Power of the Poor in History*, tr. Robert R. Barr (Maryknoll, NY: Orbis Books, 1983), selection reprinted in *World Philosophy: A Text with Readings*, ed. Robert C. Solomon and Kathleen M. Higgins (New York: McGraw Hill, 1995), pp. 239-243. Bartolome de las Casas, *The Devastation of the Indies*, tr. John Phillips, London, 1656, selection reprinted in *Social and Political Philosophy*, 2nd ed., ed. James Sterba (Belmont, CA: Wadsworth, 1998), pp. 166-168.

Glossary/Index

Note: Authors whose names appear without dates are contemporaries.